OTHER BOOKS BY HERB SNITZER

The New York I Know (with Marya Mannes)
Living at Summerhill
Today Is for Children; Numbers Can Wait

Reprise

THE EXTRAORDINARY
REVIVAL OF EARLY MUSIC

Reprise

THE EXTRAORDINARY
REVIVAL OF EARLY MUSIC

Joel Cohen & Herb Snitzer

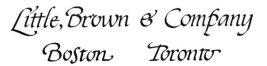

Little, Brown & Company

Boston   Toronto

FIRST EDITION

Library of Congress Cataloging in Publication Data

Cohen, Joel.
  Reprise: the extraordinary revival of early music.
  Includes index.
  1. Musicians — Biography. 2. Music — 500 – 1400 —
Performance. 3. Music — 15th century — Performance.
4. Music — 16th century — Performance. 5. Music — 17th
century — Performance. 6. Music — 18th century — Perform-
ance. I. Snitzer, Herb. II. Title.
ML394.C63 1985   780′.9   85-192
ISBN 0-316-15037-1

Calligraphy by John W. Cataldo

DESIGNED BY JEANNE F. ABBOUD

BP

Published simultaneously in Canada
by Little, Brown & Company (Canada) Limited

PRINTED IN THE UNITED STATES OF AMERICA

For Noah

JOEL COHEN

❧

To Lisa, Laura, Sigrid, and Susan,
daughters all, central and important to my life

HERB SNITZER

Contents

	Prelude: Some Questions Answered	xi
	Acknowledgments	xv
I	The Avant-garde of the Distant Past	3
II	Origins	11
III	Arnold Dolmetsch	18
IV	Early Twentieth Century	23
V	Noah Greenberg	30
VI	Thomas Binkley	38
VII	Baroque Renewal	46
VIII	The Harnoncourts and Concentus Musicus	51
IX	The Kuijkens	56
X	Frans Brüggen	61
XI	Gustav Leonhardt	67
XII	Singers, or the Main Difficulty	73
XIII	Amateurs	85
XIV	Authenticity	90
XV	Conclusions: Does the Past Have a Future?	96
	And Now the Players	103
	Glossary	217
	Index	223

Note: *Reprise* is very much a collaboration by the two authors.
Joel Cohen wrote the text; Herb Snitzer produced the photographs;
and together they prepared the captions.

Prelude: Some Questions Answered

"WHAT KIND OF MUSIC DO EARLY MUSIC PEOPLE PLAY?"

The answer, self-evident as it may seem to the little world that includes harpsichordists and chifonie players, is perhaps less obvious to those on the outside, and with good reason. In some sense, any music more than a few years old is "early" music: why then establish a special category of performance, separate from the usual kinds of classical music activity, which in any case is mainly involved with music of the past?

The specialness of early music owes as much, as we shall see, to its modern-day human context and to its very contemporary attitudes as it does to its repertoires. But just for the record, the musicians we will be talking about in this book confine themselves in the main to music written before the nineteenth century. The movement we are discussing involves music from the Middle Ages, the Renaissance, the Baroque, and the early classical periods in music history: from (roughly) the years 1100 to 1800. The main currents of music history during those centuries can be traced by the curious reader via any number of modern-day books on the subject. What these very diverse epochs all have in common is their distance from our own musical culture. The direct connection from master to student, from composer to disciple, which informs our understanding of the recent past, has been lost or broken in the case of very old music. Mahler taught his symphonies to Bruno Walter, who transmitted them to the mid-twentieth century. No such living tradition informs our performances of Palestrina or Pergolesi; and the early music movement has chosen to go very far back in time, not just in spite of the gaps in transmission, but also because of them.

The early music movement, then, can be delimited by describing the compositions it performs. But defining the repertoire that the movement has claimed as its own is only a small part of the story. After all, some of the movement's favorite works are also part of the concert-hall mainstream. Pianists and big modern orchestras and large sopranos *also* perform the music of Bach. Bach will always be Bach, but when he is performed by Horowitz, is he early music? We tend to think not. Early music is a special, wonderful, but limiting category of modern performance practice. It is a *way* of approaching the past, but it is not the past itself. Early music is not the Middle Ages; it is not the Renaissance; and it is not the Baroque. And so, the best answer to the question that began this discursion is a circular one: early music people play early music! The repertoires so treated have nonetheless benefited mightily — some had well-nigh vanished from the realm of the living until the movement began to apply its mouth-to-mouth resuscitation techniques to them.

Therefore, long live the early music movement. But if you were hoping to find a course in music history between the covers of this book, you had better backtrack. Our subject is closely related to music history, but distinct from it.

We are, of course, aware that the dulcian and the isorhythmic motet are no longer the common household objects that they never were; and so, to minimize any potential difficulties with specialized lingo, we have included a glossary of musical terms and of proper names at the end of this work.

"What Are You Trying to Do?"

When one looks at early music record covers and tape cassettes, one often sees fifteenth-century woodcuts of angels and cherubs, or reproductions of tranquil seascapes or country vistas. All well and good, up to a point, but where are the artists?

Who are the people who play early music? Would other people care to know them? Are there unknowns in this world as well as "stars" who thrill audiences with their talents and musical insights?

It is to answer those questions that we conceived of this book. We wanted to show real people making music, early music people playing early music. This book is our way of asking you, the reader-viewer, to stop and think about the people you will read about in the text and see in the photographs. In a world that seems to grow more and more indifferent to human need, a world where destruction seems to outpace creation, these musicians create music for anyone interested in enjoying, hearing, and growing from the experience. We bring you what they continually discover about their art and their world, connecting you with that world through our words and our photographs.

"How Come We're Not in the Book?"

The phone rang. "How come we're not in the book?" queried the gifted young violinist, wife and musical partner to an active and prominent practitioner of the harpsichord. The word was out. The odors of springtime suddenly grew faint, and a black cloud became visible in a distant corner of the sky.

Dear friends, dear colleagues, dear coworkers who toil for months and years at the frontiers of musical knowledge only to have some nincompoop music critic dismiss your life's effort with an ignorant paragraph or two—we hope you weren't counting on revenge at last once this book came out. This work is not the Last Judgment; it isn't even *Grove's* or *Baker's*. There is no way to "cover" the whole field of endeavor in an exhaustive manner, and we haven't even tried. This book is a personal appreciation of some (but not all) of the important musicians in the early music field, and of some (but not all) of the aesthetic and human implications of the work all of us do. If you are not mentioned by name, you are here anyway in spirit. If your picture is missing and you discover the image of some rival, more or less famous, more or less gifted than you, staring out at you, please forbear! Remember that *pars per totam*. Less is more. And the quality of mercy is not strained . . .

We speak of mercy, not justice, because inevitably there will be errors, omissions, and mistaken opinions in a work such as this one. Such faults are entirely the responsibility of the authors, but the forgiveness is yours to proffer. Let's remain friends, and let's work together to make our little field of specialized activity reach across boundaries and fill the whole cosmos with the sounds of renewal and rebirth.

Joel Cohen and Herb Snitzer

Acknowledgments

MANY people deserve thanks for helping this work to take shape. Close to us from the beginning to the end of this project was Ann Sleeper of Little, Brown and Company. Her initial interest in our idea and her continued guidance of our work at every stage have provided us with the structure we needed to do our work.

Institutions and organizations gave generously of their time and human resources to help us along. We would like to thank the New England Conservatory of Music, the Early Instruments Collection of the Museum of Fine Arts, Boston, the Boston Early Music Festival, the Utrecht Early Music Festival, and Aaron and Gorden Concert Management.

Many friends and colleagues of Herb Snitzer helped out along the way. Rick and Louise Treitman started him off on his search. Support came from Ed and Gail Snitzer; Joe and Lil Weiss; fellow photographers Jerry Berendt and John Sandhaus; Don Russell and the Crimson Group. All made the photographer's task easier.

Our warmest thanks go to the many gifted musicians who freely gave of their time and energy to help realize this project. The subjects of the photographs will find their names, for the most part, in the captions. Those who helped formulate the ideas expressed in the body of the text may or may not be mentioned directly therein. The early music field is a small one, and many of us get to say hello to one another at frequent intervals.

The author of the text would like to thank those colleagues and friends with whom he has shared more than the time of day; they have, at various occasions over the last several years, been willing to tell him some of their ideas about early music and its performance. Some of them knew that they were being interviewed for this book; others did not, because we ourselves did not yet know that we were about to embark on the venture.

Their collective wisdom and insight have inspired many of the thoughts in the following pages. As for the foolishness that the reader is bound to find as well — that part of the whole is entirely our own responsibility.

Thanks, then, for their time and their thoughts, to Anne Azéma, Ben Bagby, Julianne Baird, Thomas Binkley, Frans Brüggen, René Clemencic, Hugues Cuénod, Mark Deller, John Gibbons, Christiane Jaccottet, Michael and Kay Jaffee, Laura Jeppesen, Emma Kirkby, Sigiswald Kuijken, Esther Lamandier, Marie Leonhardt, Carol Lieberman, Jean-Claude Malgoire, Victor Mattfeld, Marcel Peres, Joshua Rifkin, Anthony Rooley, Janine Rubinlicht, Jordi Savall, Fawzi Sayeb, Jaap Schroeder, Robert Spencer, Daniel Stepner, Eric Tappy, David Thomas, Barbara Thornton, James Tyler, John Tyson, Friedrich von Huene, Andrea von Ramm, and a host of other fine musicians whose paths crossed ours during the preparation of this book.

A special thought, too, for three extraordinary people whose music continues to resonate strongly within us: Nadia Boulanger, Alfred Deller, and Noah Greenberg.

Photographs on pages xvii – xxviii

ANDREA VON RAMM

GUSTAV LEONHARDT

MARION VERBRÜGGEN

SHEILA BEARDSLEE

VADIM STRUKHOV AND
SOPHIE BOULIN

ANNER BYLSMA

JOHN GIBBONS

MARY UTIGER

ANDREW PARROTT

NIGEL NORTH

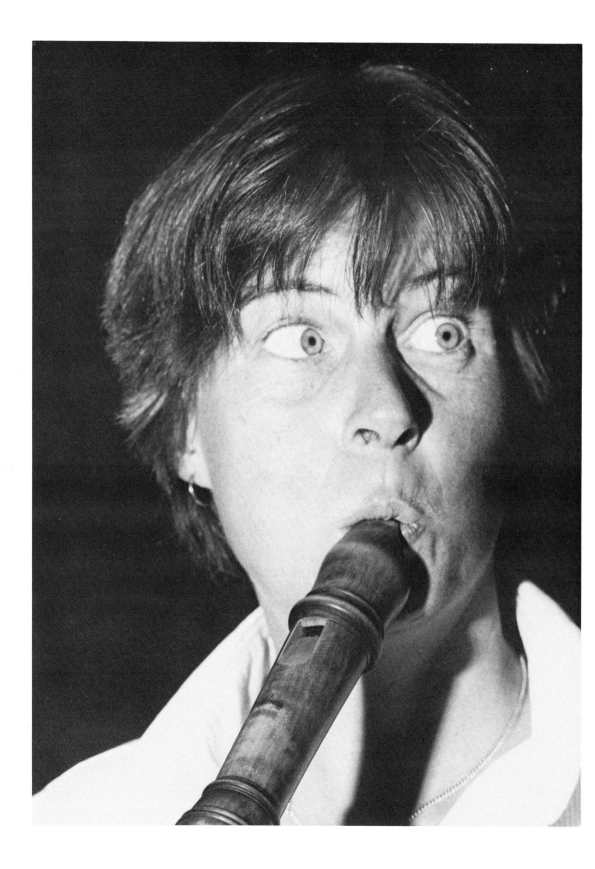

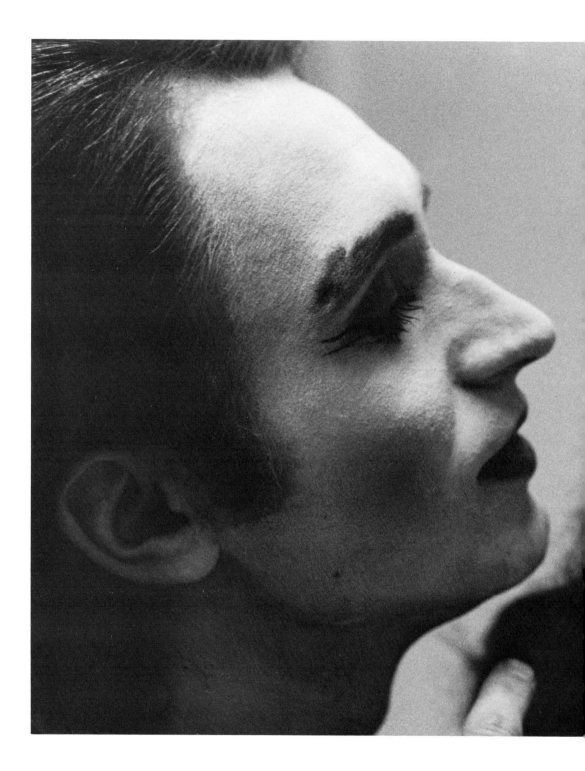

Reprise

THE EXTRAORDINARY
REVIVAL OF EARLY MUSIC

I

The Avant-garde of the Distant Past

IN the autumn of 1976 the all-music radio station that broadcasts on the FM band throughout France made a switchover in programming policy. What had once been a cautious, conservative "classical" station (lots of Chopin and Fauré) suddenly inundated the airwaves with a slew of unfamiliar musical styles and interpreters. Prominent in the new program schedules, alongside contemporary and ethnic music, were large doses of works from the distant past, performed by the likes of Gustav Leonhardt, Nikolaus Harnoncourt, Andrea von Ramm, and other outstanding early music specialists. For the first time, the French could hear quantities of Guillaume de Machaut and Johann Sebastian Bach and Claudio Monteverdi, performed with the true vocal and instrumental colors of earlier centuries.

The brickbats began flying only a few weeks after the new programming policy went into effect. Letters and phone calls poured into the station protesting the changeover from familiar music and familiar performers. Columns of newsprint filled up with indignant editorials defending the sacred traditions of French musical taste against the inroads of foreign corruption ("We don't need foreigners to teach us about our own music," barked one music critic; an

American early music ensemble had broadcast a series on Josquin des Prez). Hints of Marxist subversion circulated freely in the ultra-right-wing press.

Unable to contain his anger, Doctor Zwang, a disgruntled psychiatrist, published a pamphlet defending the "legal" pitch for performing Bach (he meant the current, twentieth-century norm), and calling the most eminent standard-bearers of the early music revival by every name under the sun. ("Can you imagine!" violinist Marie Leonhardt was overheard to remark. "Calling Harnoncourt a toad! That's really an exaggeration.")

This "war of the airwaves" (as the controversy came to be called) was fought with a fervor recalling the scandals attending the premieres of revolutionary works like *Le sacre du printemps* or *Pierrot Lunaire* three generations earlier. This time the villains were not named Stravinsky and Schoenberg, but Couperin and Kuijken, Vivaldi and Brüggen. A new avant-garde, the avant-garde of the distant past, had been officially recognized and had received its baptism in fire.

Unsuspecting, the French public had been dragged into a confrontation. In their characteristically excitable way, they were reacting (a few years later than audiences in northern Europe and America) to one of the oddest, yet most endearing, phenomena of modern times: the rush toward "early" music — not simply the Mozart-to-Debussy sliver of the past that had already been enshrined by our cultural institutions, but the more *distant* past, that part of our heritage which had long since passed out of our ken. The familiar classics of the symphony orchestras and the opera houses and the piano recitals in fact represent only a tiny portion of what Western music has been across the centuries. From the Middle Ages to the late eighteenth century (the point at which our "standard" repertoire begins) the composers of the European continent poured forth untold thousands of musical works. The heritage of music is incomparably larger, and incomparably richer, than the tiny segment that has generally been made available to us. And many forgotten compositions of the Medieval, the Renaissance, and the Baroque periods probe as deeply into the hidden corners of the human soul and offer as much spiritual consolation and insight (not to mention just plain fun) as the more familiar masterpieces of the Romantic era. Like the bored and indifferent tour guides who herd tourist groups around the châteaux of the Loire valley, the official guardians of our musical patrimony had been showing only a few of the rooms. A lot of the best stuff was being kept under lock and key upstairs, where no one had looked at it for years and years.

Gradually, the travelers to Music Castle have been learning not to trust the official guided tours. They have been walking upstairs on their own and turning the latchkeys of long-sealed-off chambers. The place is full of treasure! Persistent explorers have been rediscovering the world of Medieval vocal polyphony, of Renaissance viol consorts, of early Baroque opera, of French harpsichord music, and of a hundred other far-removed yet vitally engrossing repertoires.

Even the furniture on the ground floor has been cleaned off and given a fresh coat of varnish. The early music of the "official" tradition (the works we already know from the later parts of the eighteenth century) has been reexamined and redefined by a new generation of specialists who perform on instruments of the period (or carefully made copies) and who apply the techniques of sound production, phrasing, and articulation appropriate to the pre-Romantic era.

The controversy surrounding the music of the distant past has not been confined to France alone. The thin, quiet sounds of lutes, recorders, and Baroque violins have not been every modern music lover's cup of tea. And many a conservatory professor, newpaper journalist, or member of the audience has been heard to cry "Foul!" on being confronted with the unfamiliar ways of the early music world.

Now, it was never considered a very urgent matter to study and perform the music of old — at least not until the nineteenth century. Composers always wrote for the music lovers of their own time and place: neither they nor their public had more than a vague notion of much music older than themselves. Music was by and large an art without a past. In sixteenth-century Italy, for example, a madrigal thirty years old was considered antiquated and a subject for derision.

In seventeenth-century England, the lutenist John Dowland complained bitterly that musical fashion had passed him by; he was not yet fifty at the time. In eighteenth-century Austria, Wolfgang Amadeus Mozart, like every other composer of his day, turned out new operas and new concerti because his public demanded the stimulation of a constantly renewed, contemporary repertoire.

In fact, the world of art music prior to the Romantic era had many things in common with the popular music industry of our own time.* From the troubadours of twelfth-century Provence to Franz Joseph Haydn in the eighteenth century the patterns of creation, diffusion, and appreciation were very similar: musical works were conceived for a moment, for a given time and place. They had their day in the sun, eventually fell into disuse and neglect, and were replaced by newer and more fashionable products.

Our own peculiarly schizoid age has a much more ambivalent attitude toward the past and its great works of art. On the one hand, the terrifying rate of technological change that characterizes our society makes anything more than fifteen minutes old seem outdated; on the other hand, no age before ours has been so conservative and backward-looking when it comes to questions of taste in art music. The works of living composers of "serious" music usually interest only a handful of people, and the attention of the public at large for art music tends to focus on a small number of established masterpieces from the late eighteenth through the early twentieth centuries.

No longer does the public for "classical" music rush out to buy the latest volume of freshly composed madrigals, hot off the printing presses. No longer do café musicians play hit tunes from the season's most successful operas, as they did during Mozart's day. Instead, we treat the concert-hall experience as something not far removed from church attendance: as an opportunity to contemplate eternal, im-

---

* We are talking about *Western* music: our nervous civilization changes fashions in the arts faster than average for this planet. China and India, too, have their high cultures, but the ways their music and art evolved over the centuries differ significantly from our own, Euro-American, patterns.

[6]

movable values (or to doze off, depending on our current relationship to things Eternal).

The tendency to replace Religion with Art began, I think, in the nineteenth century. From Shelley to Ruskin, a current of Romantic thought demanded of the artist that he be a kind of moral prophet, forging new values for all of mankind. No wonder the young rebels of the twentieth century took to Cubism and country dancing — they couldn't stand the pressure to be so unremittingly holy. The Romantic-modern idea of artist-as-priest goes hand in hand with the canonization of certain works as official "masterpieces": every religion needs a Bible.

Such a quasi-religious reverence toward a fossilized musical repertoire (and the whole world of performance values, social codes, and marketing techniques that the repertoire has dragged along with it) is unique to modern times. The whole concept of the public concert is a modern one. And in a society dominated by commercial values, music has become a commodity just like anything else. Although many music lovers would be hard-pressed to admit it, their favorite conductor or violinist has gained fame in part through skillful management and publicity. And our need for a canonized body of musical masterpieces from the past characterizes us just as strongly as our opposite infatuation with speed and technological gadgetry.

Most of us accept the idea of the "standard" repertoire, consisting predominantly of works from the past, as something entirely normal, since we have never experienced anything else in the world of "classical" music. But within the musical community, an important minority has been rebelling against the canons of official music making since the early years of this century. Not all the malcontents were yearning to open the locked rooms of the castle. Quite a few, in fact, were itching to burn the old place down.

Some violent forms of protest against the classical music establishment sprang up in the years just after World War I; the protesters were composers, and they rebelled against the conventional musical wisdom of the day by destroying the accepted protocols of musical composition and by creating new, often jarring, and barely comprehensible forms of musical expression.

[7]

The wave of avant-gardism that swept across Europe during those years was (and is) a striking indictment of the malaise in our cultural establishment. Many of the avant-garde modernists in music and the other arts were resolutely futuristic and scornful of the past — a not unsurprising attitude, given the deadening effects of too much standardization and repetition on our creative spirit.

But among the modernists there were some (and those not the least influential) who rebelled against the recent past by turning to a still more distant yesterday for inspiration. Ezra Pound's translations of troubadours' poetry, William Butler Yeats's reworkings of old Celtic myths, Igor Stravinsky's and Paul Hindemith's use of neo-Bachian counterpoint — these, too, were ways of rejecting the aesthetic norms of the day. Turning toward the distant past became another means of escaping from conventionally imposed standards.

A composer can break with tradition relatively easily; he can write some new works that contain standards and ideas of their own. A performer is more limited. In Europe and America, a "classical" musician is usually someone who transmits the musical thought of another — a regrettable state of affairs, perhaps, but it is simply so. And so a performer may have a harder time than a composer in expressing his own personal values, his own artistic center through his work — especially if he feels himself to be out of step with the prevailing ethos that surrounds him.

One way for a performer to break out of the mold (if that is what he wants to do) is to specialize in the interpretation of contemporary music; that has been a solution for many fine musicians of our time. The most normal and plausible of musical destinies, in fact, has always been to perform the music of one's own day. Only in the twentieth century has playing "modern" music come to signify something rather marginal and off the track.

For many reasons, however, contemporary performers have generally tended to avoid prolonged contact with the music of their own time. Like the listening public at large, the performers' world has been slow to accept the thorny, hermetic products of the contemporary avant-garde into its bosom. One can feel alienated from the dominant values of the concert world without being simultaneously drawn toward the modernist avant-garde and *its* values.

Here is at least a partial explanation of the movement toward the performance of early music. Like the audiences who flock to early music concerts, the performers have been charmed by the intrinsic beauty and power of these repertoires; like the public, the players have fallen in love with the tranquil eloquence of old instruments and playing styles.

For the players, however, there are even deeper motivations for hitching one's career wagon to the early music star. The most important reason, I believe, for deciding to specialize in such an odd thing as the music of the distant past is to define one's own self in the here and now. Like those in the modernist camp, the early music performers often find themselves in opposition to the prevailing values of the day. (This opposition, by the way, has no necessary connection with political engagement; gambists and shawm players range all the way up and down the political spectrum, just like everyone else.) The finest performers in this field have had to stake out their own territory, have had to create their own values and standards. They needed to do so to make their music come out the right way; and they needed to make the music come out the right way because the things they had earlier been trained to hear and do did not rest well in their souls.* The decision to make early music one's life has to do above all

---

* "How the hell are *they* so sure they're doing it the right way!" snorted Mr. Grumpus, as he threw this book to the floor. Then he got up and put on his favorite recording: Heifetz playing Bach's "Air on the G string."

You can't argue with pleasure.

Some musicians, though, felt irreducibly alienated from the prevailing ways of the modern concert hall. You can't argue that feeling away, either. The old treatises, the careful reproductions of historical instruments, the scholarly studies — these things gave many early music performers an objective confirmation of that which they had been intuiting already. Most important, scholarly knowledge and research have created a psychic space for self-affirmation. A performer can say, "I'm me, not you, and so I'll play the music this way and not that."

Still, Mr. Grumpus does have a point; we aren't as sure as all that about absolute historical veracity. Early music performance is like any other skilled craft; you can follow the rules only so far, and then you are on your own.

with finding one's place in the confused and tumultuous modern age. We pay the strongest and most intensely detailed attention imaginable to the music of the distant past in order to define ourselves with greater truth and clarity in the here and now. Quoth Nikolaus Harnoncourt: "We make music in the present, totally, and as living, breathing people of our own time."

The word "authenticity" is much bandied about these days in early music circles. It is an unfortunate buzzword, since its current meaning in musical circles — see Chapter XIV — is too narrow. The word has far deeper resonances than current usage tends to permit. You will not, therefore, find it popping up very often in the pages of this book, despite its regrettable and current popularity. But there is a way in which "authenticity" in the deepest sense does apply to this musical context. In the human situations that this book's photographs depict, the struggle to do well, the boredom of waiting, the fun of success — in these images of a performing generation, you can see the authenticity of creative enterprise.

As the twentieth century lurches and heaves toward its final decade, uncertain whether life or death is its goal, every sign of hope and renewal has more than ordinary importance. Opening the locked rooms in the castle of music may seem to some a trivial activity as our planet prepares for war. Perhaps, though, the loving respect and careful nurturing that are nearly everywhere in the early music movement can find their place, and have their influence, in the world outside. May the energies released by the avant-garde of the distant past help us point the way toward a more humane and peaceful future!

II

Origins

*T*HE old prints and manuscripts lay quietly on library shelves; the music they contained was as still and empty as death. For unlike any of the plastic arts, music needs the active intervention of human concern and care to have any effect or meaning at all. A painting by Titian *is* the canvas and the colors which the artist produced. A motet by Roland de Lassus is *not* its musical notation. The notes on paper, without the mediation of sound (or at the very least, of a score-reader to imagine the sound), cannot really be said to have an existence; at least not in the same sense as any physical *objet d'art*.

And so the musical sources languished while so many other artifacts of the past managed to survive — painting, furniture, sculpture, jewelry, architecture, and urban space — and to continue influencing the consciousness of modern man. The stones of Venice, crumbling slowly into the lagoon, still are present in the lives of thousands even today. The motets and madrigals of Andrea and Giovanni Gabrieli, which made the architectural spaces of Venice resonate three and a half centuries ago, could not survive their time and place. The peeling bricks somehow cohere on the old facades of the palazzi, but the music has vanished away. . . .

Or has it? The collective efforts of a few concerned scholars, performers, and instrument makers have managed to rescue some of those glorious sounds from oblivion. What is most paradoxical (and most moving) about that enterprise is, as we have seen, its modernity. For music is by essence a living art, and even the music of the distant past, if it is to have more than a shadow existence, needs men and women of our own time to bring it to life again. And that is why the early music movement is not *primarily* the written pitches of Perotin or Luca Marenzio or Arcangelo Corelli. Those composers and their works do exist, somewhere in the history of man and the mind of God. What we are discussing in this book is something related but different: the people who have made the revival come about and who are, even more than the music they perform, the essence of the movement, the ground of its being. The early music movement cannot be defined adequately by referring only to the repertoires it performs: "To be blunt: Early Music signifies first of all people and only secondarily things." *

Who were the people who first began consciously to exhume the music of the distant past? The credit for starting the revival, or at least its Bachian side, is often given to Felix Mendelssohn. It was Mendelssohn who, in 1829, produced the first modern reconstitution of Bach's *Saint Matthew Passion;* that landmark performance went far to revive interest in old music among cultivated listeners.

True enough it is that the German Romantics rediscovered the distant past, making it part of their aesthetic ideology. The early music movement, though, has roots even farther back, in the age of the Enlightenment. In 1726, a group of musicians, professionals and well-born amateurs, united to form the Academy of Vocal Music in London; the proclaimed goal of these notables (who included Giovanni Battista Bononcini, Francesco Geminiani, and Samuel Wesley) was "to restore ancient church music." Their field of endeavor was clarified still further in 1731: "By the compositions of the Ancients

* Laurence Dreyfus, "Early Music Defended against Its Devotees: A Theory of Historical Performance in the Twentieth Century," *The Musical Quarterly* (Summer 1983).

is meant of such as lived before the end of the sixteenth century." *

Following a scandal that involved charges of plagiarism against Bononcini (and the resignation of that composer's supporting faction), the remaining nucleus regrouped, calling itself the Academy of Ancient Music. The composer John Christopher Pepusch (who is best remembered for harmonizing the tunes in John Gay's *Beggar's Opera*) and the famed music historian John Hawkins were active in this academy, which possessed an extensive library and offered a series of subscription concerts to its members.

Disbanded in 1792, the Academy of Ancient Music was not the only "early music" organization prominent in London life. The Earl of Sandwich founded the Concert of Antient Music in 1776; a work had to be at least twenty years old in order to be considered for performance at one of the concerts, which centered around the music of George Frideric Handel; in a daring move, some late works of Mozart were introduced around 1826! A memoir from the year 1803 accuses the concert programs of "want of variety" and "total discouragement of living genius"—familiar strictures against early music concerts ever since. This concert society was at any rate respectable beyond reproach; Handel, then as now, was the most uncontroversial of the great masters. Perhaps out of Germanic solidarity, perhaps to console himself for the loss of the American colonies, George III became a regular subscriber in 1785. No California hippies in this crew!**

A working-man's equivalent of these noble academies was the Madrigal Society, "mostly mechanics; some weavers from Spitalfields, others of various trades and occupations."† Founded in

---

* "London," *The New Grove's Dictionary of Music and Musicians* (London, 1980), vol. XI, p. 194.

** These London academies signaled the beginnings of two trends, in fact: on the one hand, the early music movement, with its abiding curiosity about the distant past; and on the other, the canonization of a standard repertoire. The two tendencies, now fairly distinct, are intermixed at this point in our narrative.

† "London," *The New Grove's Dictionary,* vol. XI, p. 194.

1741, the London society continues to this day. In a burst of modernist audacity, women were admitted to sing the soprano parts of the madrigals after the Second World War.

(Amateur sociologists may note with amusement the relegation of madrigal singing, once an aristocratic pastime, to the popular classes. The proletarization of the madrigal and the Renaissance part-song has continued to this day. While Yuppies nibble quiche and sip Chablis to the sound of Handel, your prototypical madrigal singer from Cambridge, Massachusetts still shows up for rehearsal in faded jeans and a baggy old sweater.)

In Germany, where the Idea reigns supreme, the revival of interest in early music had more to do with study than with performance. The Romantic composers did indeed make a major contribution to our modern taste by their enthusiastic championing of Bach's works. Even more vital to the movement as we know it today was the creation, largely through the labors of German scholars, of the modern discipline called Musicology.

It was the scholar Johann Nikolaus Forkel who first published a biography of Bach in 1802. More important still, he and some other university-trained thinkers of his generation began to approach music as an object of "scientific" research: using the same careful methods of observation and classification that were being applied in the natural sciences, in history, and in philology. The thorough, no-stone-unturned ways of the German university professor were trained on the most fragile and evanescent of human cognitive activities: the art of sound.

Like the early music performance movement, the discipline of musicology is a product of modern civilization. Machaut would not have known what to make of it; Palestrina would have been bewildered; and Vivaldi would have excused himself to make an urgent phone call. Even today, what the scholars do in the academy is not generally known or understood. Many a piano major, freshly arrived from some midwestern music school, finds the graduate program at Ivy League University X not to her liking or expectations. Instead of practicing her Schubert, she finds herself spending long hours before a microfilm reader, trying to sort out the different scribal hands in Oxford Canon. Misc. 213.

Meticulous analysis and comparison of musical sources were never implemented in earlier times. No one ever made a detailed study of early notational practices until the nineteenth century. And the very notion of the *Gesamtausgabe,* the complete works of a composer (or a school) based on careful research, is as much a product of the systematizing industrial age as the railroad schedule or the stamp collection.

To the German university scholars of the nineteenth century we owe modern editions of Giovanni Pierluigi da Palestrina, Roland de Lassus, Johann Sebastian Bach, George Frideric Handel, François Couperin, and others. More important yet, those scholars elaborated and transmitted their method of working to succeeding generations; German *Musikwissenschaft* (musical knowledge) is now to the academic music world what Christian theology was to the Middle Ages. Like theological discourse, the musicological approach has its limits and its own peculiar way of deforming reality. Like theology, it can encourage intolerance and narrowness of outlook. But systematic thought does get results. We would not be hearing all those musical treasures of the past without countless hours of archival work as a necessary prelude.

To the Germanic world we owe as well the strong link between early music and student life. The *Collegium Musicum* performing madrigals on the campus lawn somewhere in Iowa or Nebraska descends from the amateur groups that flourished in the eighteenth- and nineteenth-century universities (and in German society at large, for that matter). The original purpose of such music societies was to perform new works; but in 1908 the musicologist Hugo Riemann founded a new kind of Collegium Musicum in Leipzig. His ensemble, made up of university students, was created to perform Baroque instrumental music, and to study that music as well. The nonprofessional, student collegium, an essential part of the early music revival in Germany and America, was born; the most illustrious example of the Germanic collegium in the New World remains without question the one founded at Yale in 1943 by composer Paul Hindemith.

Nowadays every self-respecting university has its set of matched krumhorns, its recorder consort, and its anxious graduate student trying to extract in-time and in-tune performances from the department's early music ensemble. Many a current early music pro began a love affair with the past in college. If the college collegia tend to be creaky affairs, and if their scholarship-oriented directors tend to be out of touch with the values and goals of professional performers, these organizations still create a space for discovery and delectation. In the technique-oriented world of modern academia, that liberal and humanistic goal is nothing to be sneezed at.

A well-organized university system launched the German scholars into their collective enterprise; the seedling discipline of musicology (and, concurrently, amateur performances of early music) were able to grow in a favorable, encouraging environment. No such structure was available to would-be professional performers of early music. To the University, professional performance has traditionally been considered as a mechanical craft, the domain of the Conservatory. And as for the conservatories, the less said about most of them, the better, at least insofar as the performance of historical music is concerned.*

A recent and true story will make the point: a young French tenor, meeting by chance his former voice teacher in the halls of the Paris Conservatoire, was asked by the older man what he had been performing recently. "I just sang a concert of the Machaut Mass," said the tenor. "My friend," exclaimed the teacher, visibly upset, "how many times must I tell you? There's no future in that crazy modern music!" The would-be early music professional has always had a hard time convincing the mainliners to take his activities at all seriously.

By the end of the nineteenth century, there were places to go if you wanted to be a music-historical scholar. You could even associate

---

* In modern America, the university curriculum often includes music performance; but traditionally, universities shunned practical music making, even when history and theory were offered to students. From the Medieval Sorbonne to the modern state university, the European system has changed very little in this regard.

with others to perform early music in student ensembles and amateur madrigal groups. No one as yet had tried to base his entire career, his entire existence, on the music of the distant past — no one, that is, except the hero of our next chapter.

III

Arnold Dolmetsch

He looked as if he had jumped out of an Elizabethan picture . . . dressed in a mole colored velvet suit. . . . He looked charming . . . but we used to have terrible arguments. . . . He would say, "Why do you bother with such a hateful instrument as the piano? . . . " But we loved touring with them. . . . They looked enchanting in their costumes.

—REMINISCENCES OF DAME SYBIL THORNDIKE*

*T*HE theme of solitude, of one man struggling against an indifferent and even hostile outside world, recurs over and over again in the life story of a crucially important early music figure. Some of the isolation experienced by Arnold Dolmetsch (1858–1940) was due to his thorny, irascible personality. "For some decades [his] insight was confined to a tiny minority whose isolation was exacerbated by the very ferocity of his partisanship. He used to prelude his concerts with paranoid attacks on those 'imbeciles' (French pronunciation, very fierce), the professors of music, the academics, the critics, long

* Quoted in Margaret Campbell, *Dolmetsch: The Man and His Work* (Seattle, 1975), p. 168.

[18]

after these influential people had become more open to his arguments."*

Uprooted and vagabond (he was born in France of a Swiss German family, studied violin in Brussels, made harpsichords for a while in Boston, but spent most of his long career in England, where he died), Dolmetsch was in many ways the quintessential modern man. He attempted, through Herculean effort, both physical and mental, to reconstruct a private universe, seemingly to replace a shattered outside world. Dolmetsch transcribed his repertoire from the old manuscripts; he collected and learned to play (with varying degrees of skill) and then built himself many kinds of historical instruments: recorders and violins and violas da gamba and harpsichords and clavichords and lutes. He wrote extensively on every aspect of early music performance: articles, an authoritative book, extensive program annotations for his concert performances; and carried on a lively correspondence with many prominent literary and artistic personalities of his day.

He organized concert after concert, festival after festival. He begat from his own loins the key members of his performing ensembles: for the Dolmetsch children were expected to perform in their father's consorts, and the sooner the better. He wanted his personal and his artistic life to be one and the same thing, and his children suffered heavily from that desire. His view of things was monomaniacal and authoritarian.**

The True Believers of all schools and all ideologies have made deep inroads into modern history; now and then, they have done more good than harm. We can perhaps be thankful that young Arnold chose music as his life's vocation and not religion or politics.

In recent years it has become fashionable to ridicule the Dolmetsch ethos. The wayward, amateurish quality of his performances and some of his writings, his isolation from other musicians and

---

* Robert Donington, "Why Early Music?" *Early Music* (January 1983), p. 23.

** The most noted of the festivals was the one at Haslemere, Dolmetsch's home in England. Dolmetsch was estranged for fifteen years from his first daughter, Hélène; they reconciled only a few months before her death in 1919.

scholars, his tyrannical ways — all these are easy to criticize from our present-day vantage point.

We now have a small army of specialists — scholars, instrument makers, performers, music educators, concert impresarios — to do the many things that Dolmetsch tried to accomplish almost single-handedly. His failures have nothing surprising about them. What is truly extraordinary is how very *much* he was able to achieve.

Dolmetsch's book on the interpretation of Baroque music, published in 1915, was a touchstone work for many years. Many important style principles were accurately described and documented in that book; things that surprised critics and public in the 1960s and 1970s, when the "new wave" of Baroque performers began to achieve prominence, had been discovered and discussed by Dolmetsch half a century earlier.

The special role that Dolmetsch foresaw for early music in education, in family and group life, has now become part of our everyday reality. For better or for worse (I tend to think for the better) the school recorder class and the Sunday afternoon amateur consort occupy a small but significant corner of the twentieth-century cultural landscape.

> *My idea for July and August is this — to get Dolmetsch to make me a lute and to coast the South of England from Falmouth to Margate singing old English songs.*
>
> —JAMES JOYCE*

There had been scholars and antiquarians to peek now and then at old prints and manuscripts; there had been timid attempts to perform on old instruments (as the Franco-Belgian Société des Instruments Anciens, founded in 1895, did). But no one, until Dolmetsch came along, had made a serious effort to reproduce historical instruments from scratch. The young Arnold, born into a family of instrument-makers from Le Mans, and trained as a woodworker and piano craftsman, was able to make a unique contribution to the musical world. His mind was alive and probing, and his hands were skilled.

* Letter of 3 June 1904, quoted in Campbell, *Dolmetsch,* p. 157.

Dolmetsch was the first of a new kind of workman: the artisan-scholar, able to blend learning with manual dexterity in the reproduction of old instruments. The Hubbards, the Dowds, the von Huenes, and the many other contemporary craftsmen who make painstaking reproductions of early instruments are the spiritual descendants of Arnold Dolmetsch. Even the more industrialized shops, where recorders and harpsichord kits are turned out like cans of Campbell's soup, could not have come into being without the market for their wares that the Dolmetsch ethos helped to create.

> *For most people the early Haslemere festival performances conjure up visions of aesthetic young men and elderly ladies in liberty smocks and sandals.*
>
> — MARGARET CAMPBELL, *Dolmetsch*

> *I recall from the early days of my schoolboy apprenticeship at Haslemere a party of his talented family . . . and eager disciples. . . . If the roof had come down, I thought, that would have been the end of the early music movement. That was something of an exaggeration, since by then there was also [harpsichordist Wanda] Landowska; but we were not allowed in Haslemere to attribute any great merit to her or to such other few rivals as rumour presently reported.*
>
> — ROBERT DONINGTON, "WHY EARLY MUSIC?"

Marginality was an essential part of the Dolmetsch ethos; in some sense it was freely chosen. In other ways, the separateness was imposed by the outside world. Early music, or at any rate the early music life-style as espoused by the Dolmetsch family and associates, was somehow regarded as not quite sound. The Dolmetsch circle reacted to mistrust and neglect in a characteristically human way; the little crew just dug in deeper and flaunted its differences more than ever.

But even self-conscious marginality gets institutionalized in the end (as many a sixties rock star can relate). By 1929 there was a Dolmetsch Foundation. In 1937, a few years before his death, the crusty pioneer, ill and impoverished, was granted a pension — of £110 per annum! He was awarded the Croix de la Légion d'Honneur, and an honorary Doctor of Music degree from the University of Durham in the final months of his life. And the many early instrument affinity groups that began forming in the 1930s (starting with the Society of Recorder Players in 1937) owe their genesis to Dolmetsch's trailblazing activities.

The ad hoc mixture of nostalgia, scholarship, hard work, aestheticism, self-imposed marginality, amateurish *laisser aller,* and feverish dedication was to characterize much of the early music movement for many years after Dolmetsch's passing — so much so that for many in the outside world early music performance was synonymous with well-meaning ineptitude. Nowadays, the newly won professional standards of the early music community are accepted and rejoiced in with hardly a backward glance at the old, struggling days.* But we forget Dolmetsch at our peril. There really is something in the depths of the early music repertoire that invites us to change our values, to alter our lives. We need not wear funny costumes to heed that call; we had better not force our children to bend their psyches to our nostalgic will. But it might be a good thing, up to a point, to integrate the Dolmetsch ethos into our present activities. If you give it a chance, the music of the distant past will turn you around and make you into a different person. Existential change, after all, is what great art tends to be all about. Be careful as you pick up that recorder! Take care as you insert that Dowland tape into your Walkman! Do you really want to take the risk?

* A listener's account of a Dolmetsch family concert, quoted in Campbell, *Dolmetsch* (p. 232), suggests what the prevailing standards may have been: "During the first quartette Mr. Dolmetsch stopped the players, explaining that he was not satisfied with his son's entry on the recorder. 'Not incisive enough, you understand' he told us. And when the passage was repeated we were asked if we had noticed the improvement? We agreed, and the recital continued.

"Then Mr. Dolmetsch told us he proposed playing, on the lute, an ancient piece of music which was particularly difficult and he was not at all sure he could manage it! Having played it through once he was not satisfied, and asked our permission to play it a second time . . . a unique musical experience."

IV

Early Twentieth Century

*T*HE old man, blind and enfeebled, made his way onto the Jordan Hall concert stage. His hand felt for the length of string that, suspended from the stage exit, guided him to the harpsichord. As he seated himself and began to play, a recording angel in Heaven made a final annotation in a celestial ledger. The first Boston Early Music Festival, in 1981, had begun with the last public appearance in Boston of the legendary Ralph Kirkpatrick (1911–1984).

Those who make early music today know of someone like Arnold Dolmetsch from books and articles, and from the musical ways of his students and disciples. Much closer to us are those masters, now departed, whom we listened to and/or studied with in our formative years—those formidable personalities who gave concerts, made disk recordings, and taught classes during the middle third of the twentieth century.

Kirkpatrick, who taught at Yale for many years, was such a formative figure. Because he was a genuine scholar—his work on the keyboard music of Domenico Scarlatti (1685–1757) remains authoritative—but mostly because he was a real musician who thought intensely about real musical problems, he became one of the most widely admired and respected performers of his generation.

[23]

When the Boston Festival invited him to perform, the organizers were paying a debt to the past.

They were also extending an imaginary piece of string that reached back even farther than the one onstage. Kirkpatrick had been formed in part by musicians older than he. At the age of twenty, he had studied in Paris with theorist Nadia Boulanger and harpsichordist Wanda Landowska; both of those powerfully important women made a lasting contribution to the early music revival, at a time (only a few generations ago) when the distant past was not such an ordinary part of our listening experience.

Few people associate Nadia Boulanger (1887–1979) with the performance of early music. She is much better known as a teacher of theory and composition; in America especially, she gained fame as the woman who trained many of our native twentieth-century composers. She was, in fact, not much of an early music specialist, if you measure her specific historical knowledge by current standards. Yet she devoted much of her performing career to the music of the distant past, with results that were absolutely extraordinary for the period (and, sometimes, for any period). Profoundly conservative in many ways, she nonetheless maintained throughout her career a passionate interest in new and unfamiliar music. Her vast personal library was full of early music scores. The unsuspecting theory pupil was betimes asked, at the beginning of his lesson, to sight-read a motet by Josquin des Prez or a chanson by Clément Janequin (in the original clefs, of course). Only then would Mademoiselle proceed to pick out the mistakes in his laboriously prepared harmony exercises.

The 1937 Boulanger-directed recordings of Monteverdi madrigals (complete with her piano continuo) are still unsurpassed in their apprehension of the composer's harmonic palette and sense of rhetorical gesture. Her little recorded anthology of French vocal music contains some exquisitely sensitive renderings of Renaissance and Baroque miniatures. A nearly unobtainable recording that she directed (in the early 1950s) of music by seventeeth-century composer Marc-Antoine Charpentier is still miraculously fresh and vital. While everyone else was performing French Baroque music as though it were Brahms, Boulanger opted for light singing voices, quick, light bowstrokes, and crisp, dancing rhythms. We can still, in the eighties, be subjected to "official" performances of Baroque works that are far less alive and insightful than Boulanger's pioneer readings made years ago.

Like Nadia Boulanger, Wanda Landowska (1879–1959) was blessed with a long lifespan and an active, influential career. She gave her first harpsichord concert in 1903, and recorded her complete set of Bach's *Well-Tempered Clavier* nearly half a century later; those latter recordings were offered as membership premiums by the Book-of-the-Month Club during the 1950s. We are talking, then, about a performer whose sphere of influence extended far beyond the still-tiny early music community of her day. While the Dolmetschniks proselytized among amateur musicians and in literary-artistic circles, Landowska was giving solo recitals in the same halls, and for the same audiences, as the famous violinists and pianists of those times. Not for her the timid tinkle of some antique keyboard: the harpsichords she played (built to her specifications by the French piano firm, Pleyel) were robust, metal-cast contraptions. The Pleyels she made famous through concerts and recordings were meant to fill large halls with plenty of noise; built inside with modern piano technology, they also contained almost as many oddball voicing contraptions as the Japanese electrical keyboards now invading our department stores. The Pleyels boomed in the bass and boinked in the treble like the true pieces of late Victoriana that they were.

The purists, the few that existed, turned up their noses; but for the average concertgoer Landowska was the apostle of early music on earth — and the Pleyel was a harpsichord.

In retrospect, the majority opinion was correct on both scores, at least up to a point. The metal monster wasn't really a harpsichord, but it wasn't quite a piano either. And Landowska herself, despite the cult of personality that surrounded her (as it surrounded Arnold Dolmetsch) was a superbly insightful musician after all. The Romantic sweep, the extravagant gesture that she favored on the concert stage may have been derived from nineteenth-century pianism. Nonetheless, her approach worked very well in much Baroque music. The dry-as-dust, just-play-the-notes manner of the forties and fifties Baroque players was, as we now see, hopelessly wide of the mark. The music of the distant past clearly demands emotion and expressive phrasing. Landowska seems closer to the true spirit of those repertoires than many a player of the generation that came after.

Listen again (if you can find the reissue on RCA) to Landowska's old and famous 78-rpm performance of a Vivaldi violin concerto transcribed by J. S. Bach, and further reworked by W. L. The things that drove the audiences wild, and the purists crazy, are all there: Technicolor registrations, arbitrary changes of tempo and octave, intensely personalized phrasing. But the control! The rhythmic energy! The sense of dramatic gesture! It's not the Bach of the 1980s (nor is it in many respects the Bach of the 1730s), but it is still marvelous performance. More than that, it is performance connected in some vitally important ways with the original musical text, despite certain distortions and errors of taste. Landowska could make that Pleyel do almost anything: it was even, at her hands, capable of playing early music.

Landowska was a star, a well-known concert personality; her passionate advocacy of Baroque keyboard music spilled over into the general consciousness of the concertgoing public. There was no such public defender of Medieval and Renaissance music in the concert mainstream until at least the 1950s, when Alfred Deller, Noah Greenberg, and, a few years later, David Munrow, director of the Early Music Consort of London, arrived on the scene.

Medieval and Renaissance music never was, and probably never will be, as popular, as widely accepted, as the well-known works of the Baroque era. Even today, with the early music revival in full bloom, the number of professional ensembles dealing with very distant repertoires is small compared with the many performers who specialize in Baroque music. The newborn early music Establishment (yes, Virginia, there is now an Establishment in this once-marginal field) favors familiar music. America's only major early music festival, for example, spends most of its entrepreneurial energy (and most of its money) on Baroque opera; and the remainder of its concert offerings are heavily weighted toward seventeenth- and eighteenth-century repertoires.

Things are relatively harder, even now, for the Medieval-Renaissance performer than for her Baroque-leaning colleagues: the market for her wares is smaller, and the degree of recognition she can hope to achieve is not large. She persists (I imagine) because she is in love with the music itself. She finds in a mass by fifteenth-century Guillaume Dufay or a madrigal by sixteenth-century Cipriano de Rore the same kinds of spiritual fulfillment that others obtain from Haydn quartets or Handel arias.

It requires courage and independence to defend repertoires that the world considers secondary, trivial, or just too unfamiliar. Safford Cape (1906–1973) never became famous like Landowska or Kirkpatrick. His ensemble, the Pro Musica Antiqua of Brussels, which he founded in the 1930s, was known primarily to a small group of scholars and specialists. He nonetheless promoted the Medieval and Renaissance repertoires for many years, using period instruments and light, clear vocal colors. Like many who have been drawn to pre-Baroque music, the Denver-born Cape was an American transplanted to Europe. (Others who made the reverse migration include Thomas Binkley, Sterling Jones, and Richard Levitt of the Studio der Fruehen Musik; lutenists James Tyler and Hopkinson Smith; and Barbara Thornton and Ben Bagby of the Cologne-based Sequentia ensemble.* America tends to eject its Renaissance mavens back into the Old World.)

Cape's musicians were perhaps most successful when they sang French-language texts; in some other repertoires, certain limitations of instrumental and vocal technique prevented the ordinary listener from entering fully into the spirit of the music. And the Brussels ensemble cultivated a quiet, inward style, contrasting most sharply with the dominant ethos of the modern concert world. Not until

* For the Studio der Fruehen Musik see Chapter VI; for the Sequentia ensemble see the Photograph Section.

Noah Greenberg and David Munrow began emphasizing the brilliant, extrovert sides of Renaissance music did the general public begin to pay much heed.

Any music of the past that we perform today reflects our own values and our own priorities. And since we know so little about how Medieval and Renaissance music was performed, our interpretive choices involve a still higher degree of subjectivity — more so than when we play music closer to us in time.

Medieval-Renaissance performers often choose the coloring that suits their own training and their own life-styles. Married to the daughter of a famous Belgian musicologist, Cape was also wedded to the cautious, mild-mannered approach of the university classroom. Both the strengths and the weaknesses of the Brussels Pro Musica Antiqua derived in large part from the academic style of dealing with the world.

For a few years, from the late fifties to the early seventies, another way of presenting that music was in vogue. The New York Pro Musica and the Early Music Consort of London (directed by Greenberg and Munrow, respectively) won public acclaim by stressing showmanship and brilliance in the same repertoires where Cape had found delicacy and sobriety. But the earnest, pedagogical vein of Medieval-Renaissance performance continued in the sixties and seventies with Konrad Ruhland's Capella Antiqua in Munich. Uncompromisingly straightforward in his concert and recorded programs, Ruhland made his mark by producing clean, transparent, superbly linear performances of choral polyphony: this at a time in America when numerous semiprofessional ensembles, dealing in music of the same periods, were hitting the tambourines for all they were worth.

Even now, in the eighties, schools of thought diverge concerning the best way to approach Medieval and Renaissance music in modern performance. The Greenberg-Munrow constellation of values (which we will be discussing in the following chapter) seems to be on the wane, and young ensembles now tend to take an opposite tack: they program longer, denser works. They favor sparse, uncrowded instrumentation. And they frequently adopt a sober, sometimes even a somber, concert manner. The ethos of Cape's Brussels Pro Musica, which had been in wide disfavor during the Greenberg-Munrow ascendancy, is now viewed in a much more friendly light.

What we are discussing, of course, is artistic politics in the twentieth century, and only secondarily the music of the distant past itself. The modern performer can plan his Renaissance concert program many ways. He can choose to perform entertainment music, or he can plan a recital only of dense, probing works. He can demonstrate many possible instrumental colors, or he can stick to a few. He can search out one strain of Renaissance musical expression, or he can create a synthetic panorama of different genres. The music is there, in its myriad possibilities of renewal and reinterpretation; you will choose from among those possibilities the ones which suit your needs, your training, your goals — and your unconscious!

We strive, of course, for fidelity to the past. One cannot reinvent history out of whole cloth. Nonetheless, many bitter discussions about "authenticity" could be avoided if the participants had a greater sense of their own, contemporary mindset. What is fashionable now in early music circles may be completely *démodé* a generation hence. And even that which is currently out of style may have some measure of musical and human truth. We can apprehend the musical past only in a partial, limited way; thankfully, those who came before us, and those who will come after, heard and felt, and will hear and feel, other things in early music than we do now. We are all extending pieces of string to each other. The cords reach forward and back, and they may, if we allow them, take us to a place where the lost music we are attempting to rediscover can finally be found again.

V

Noah Greenberg

How can you speak with critical detachment of a man who has been your more-or-less conscious role model for many years? It was in large part because of Noah Greenberg (1919–1966) and the ensemble he founded, the New York Pro Musica, that my own life took the direction it did.

And how can you reconcile our current perspective on the Pro Musica's legacy of recorded performances — they now seem hopelessly pushed, metronomic, and off the track — with the exhilaration, the joyous gratitude felt by young musicians of my generation? For the Pro Musica's concerts and recordings led us to discover new and infinitely promising musical horizons.

Few things, in fact, seem to illustrate better the quandary of the early music specialist than the Pro Musica's old records. For if the essence of the musical past is in some sense eternal, independent of current fad and fashion, our *apprehension* of that music is very much bound up with our own, modern time.

During the Pro Musica's heyday (the late 1950s and early 1960s), the group was acclaimed for its pioneer efforts in restoring Medieval and Renaissance music to an honored place in modern musical experience; praise for the ensemble's high professional standards was just about unanimous. Today, only nineteen years after Greenberg's sudden death at the age of forty-six, hardly anybody in the field chooses to emulate the performing style the Pro Musica made famous.

Our perception of these repertoires has shifted markedly in just a few years' time. In the vast majority of today's early music ensembles, the heavy, vibrato-laden voices of Greenberg's vocal soloists would seem radically out of place. Approaches to instrumental playing, too, have changed since the old Pro Musica days — the virtuoso performances of one generation can seem like empty note-pushing to the next.

Yet Greenberg and his colleagues were first-rate professionals by the standards of their day. Unlike Dolmetsch and his circle, they were never accused of deficiencies in basic technique. Their presentations were always noted for a high degree of fluency and polish: this, in fact, was one of the ensemble's selling points on the concert circuit. Early music, thanks to the New York Pro Musica, was no longer to be the domain of uncertain amateurs.

Our own tastes have changed, have become more developed and more refined since the Pro Musica halcyon days. Ironically, our progression in taste has come about in part because of the Pro Musica's early efforts, and not just in spite of them. If their *Play of Daniel,* which catapulted the ensemble into international fame, now seems impossibly un-Medieval as we rehear the record and look at the old production photos, weirdly reminiscent of Cecil B. deMille — if that production now seems obsolete and superseded, it is all to Noah Greenberg's honor! Those efforts of a generation ago opened doors, whetted appetites, and gave many of us the urge to learn, to explore, and to achieve something in our own right.

There is a lesson in humility here for the current crop of early music performers. For, barring some kind of miracle, it is most likely that our performances, too, will age badly. We are the children of our own time; despite our laudable concern for historical accuracy and authentic performance techniques, our carefully researched interpretations of early repertoire are part of Boston or Amsterdam or Paris in the eighties, just as Pro Musica was part of New York in the fifties. The frantic tempos and pounding rhythms of Greenberg's

Josquin des Prez recall the rumble of the IRT subway as much as they do the Gothic churches of Flanders. But in twenty years our own tics and fetishes will be just as evident in the performances we have left behind.

What, then, is the lasting value of Greenberg's career? To begin an answer to that question, you must try to relive the experience of a New York Pro Musica concert, as such a concert was apprehended by educated, receptive people in the late 1950s.

First of all, imagine America in the Eisenhower years. Imagine what that period represented in terms of blandness, conformity, and the fear of appearing different or unusual.

Then imagine a performing group whose instrumentarium resembled nothing ever seen on the concert circuit; instrumentalists who manipulated these outlandish tools with facility and relish; singers with fine clear voices (sometimes more than that; the spookily beautiful timbre of countertenor Russell Oberlin has not been replicated since); and a balding, bespectacled conductor in early middle age who looked like the archetypical Jewish uncle from the Bronx.

Imagine further an ensemble whose members obviously enjoyed performing, individually and together, Greenberg's cannily composed concert programs, programs designed to sell inexperienced audiences on some very unfamiliar kinds of music. For the Pro Musica style was in general quite extroverted. Scholarship helped make up the programs, but so did the proven virtues of good old American show-biz. Typically, Pro Musica presented anthologies of Medieval and Renaissance compositions, combining works both instrumental and vocal, in a variety of genres: mass music, motets, madrigals, instrumental dances, and pieces from the lighter side of the Renaissance musical universe. In a repertoire conceived centuries before the modern concert hall was to come into being, Greenberg felt his way. He intuited what kinds of pieces would "work" in American concert halls, before nonspecialist audiences. So skillful was he in marketing the distant past that Pro Musica was able to move away from the special-interest recital and the Sunday afternoon museum lecture and into the mainstream of concert life.

And the concert life of that unheroic time was much improved as a result. It all came as an enormous breath of fresh air, a revitalizing force in the local community concert series and the officially approved exercises of symphony, opera, and ballet.

If Noah Greenberg had never existed (to paraphrase Voltaire), it would have been necessary to invent him. Early music in America had never before ventured with success into the real world. Audiences had not had a chance to hear Medieval and Renaissance works performed with a reasonable measure of craftsmanship and competence. Since we have a hard time separating the *how* from the *what* of a performance, we tend to assimilate our impressions of a given interpretation with the work itself. Generations of music-history students learned to associate the music of the distant past with creaky, out-of-tune instruments and tentative, amateurish performers. How many times did the college music majors of my generation cue up a track from the Anthologie Sonore* with the express purpose of giggling at some scandalously inept passage or other? The further implication was that the music, too, was in some way crude or inept. Medieval people sat in humid monasteries all day flagellating themselves, and the music they made was the reflection of their unenlightened mental state.

Noah and his troupe began changing those misconceptions. A very large body of music that had been considered merely curious (when it was considered at all) was now seen to be as vital and absorbing as it truly was. And Greenberg's fresh, unpretentious, no-nonsense approach to music making really did evoke the springtime of European civilization. America is still a young country, and the secular music of the Renaissance was by and large written for and performed by young people. In some ways Pro Musica's brash energy fitted areas of

---

* The Anthologie Sonore was the first attempt to put the history of music onto phonograph records. Conceived by the German musicologist Curt Sachs, a man of unusual intellectual breadth and someone who was never afraid to take risks, the project was an admirable first try. It enlisted some of the best performing groups of the thirties and forties, such as Safford Cape's Pro Musica Antiqua and the Sestetto Luca Marenzio. But it tasted like cod-liver oil to the music students who were required to ingurgitate its contents in medicinal doses. Many a lifelong hatred of early music has grown from the required-listening syllabus of a college music-history seminar.

repertoire—notably dance music and the lighter forms—better than the excessively sobersided approach in favor among the cultists of the previous generation. Greenberg had been a sailor and a union organizer before settling on a musical career. The music of the distant past was new to him, and he made it new to his public.

Less than new, alas, were the ways in which the American music business co-opted and recycled Pro Musica's formulas for success following Greenberg's untimely death.

Pro Musica itself led a harum-scarum existence for some seasons thereafter: cautious board members chose "safe" replacements for the directorial post (the brilliant Thomas Binkley was disqualified when he told the search committee that all the singers would have to retrain), and after several years of increasingly dispirited performances under music directors who lacked either the will or the knowledge to renew Pro Musica's performing style, the group disbanded. The bookings had dried up. In a few short years Pro Musica had evolved (or devolved) into institutional decrepitude. Ways of doing things that once made sense were now meaningless traditions. Pro Musica had become General Motors, and the Datsuns and Toyotas of the early music world were making their inroads into the market.

Tenaciously, the old ways of doing things held on, not only within that ensemble, but also in the American performance world outside. Concert-booking agents now expected other ensembles to duplicate Pro Musica's proven formulas for success. There had to be six singers, there had to be four instruments, there had to be an ornamented recorder piece, there had to be one solo for each singer in the second half, there had to be brilliant orchestration with frequent shifts of instrumental color, et cetera et cetera. . . .* Even in the

---

* Since the late eighteenth century, composers have specified their instrumentations very precisely. Contrariwise, much Renaissance music can be transferred from one medium to another (from voices to viols, for example) without too much harm done: adaptation to the performing forces at hand was the Renaissance norm. Modern performers, too, have proved adept at reworking old musical texts for their own ensembles. But, inevitably, our adaptations have something of ourselves in them. Greenberg liked lots of instrumental color, and unusual voicings and octave doublings. One could justify some of that propensity via the writings of theoreticians like Michael Praetorius (1571–1621), who described many unusual

mid-eighties, nineteen years after Greenberg's death, the canonization of Pro Musica's tricks of the trade continues. Only recently, for
instance, an active American ensemble about to produce the *Play of
Daniel* lost a whole string of prospective bookings. The group in-
sisted on designing new costumes and sets, while many sponsors
demanded that the "original" Pro Musica costumes, still preserved in
mothballs by a special foundation set up for the purpose, be reuti-
lized. No Pro Musica costumes? Very well, no booking . . .

There is something absurd about preserving a thirteenth-century
liturgical drama in the formaldehyde of a late-1950s Broadway-cum-
Hollywood extravaganza, but who ever said modern concert life
wasn't absurd? And Noah Greenberg, the anti-Establishmentarian,
the man who was proud to be an outsider, would have been quick to
see the joke, and to laugh his long, hearty bull-laugh on seeing his
innovations and experiments become the obligatory pirouettes of
official music. What is precious about the Greenberg heritage is not
the specific decisions he made about this or that piece, not the
tinseled costumes for this or that production, not the style options
reflecting a specifically American time and place. What we need to
remember is Noah's open, generous, innovative spirit and his unflag-
ging commitment to making early music enjoyable and accessible.

Of course, in a way, it is wonderful to see how much Greenberg is
still a part of our musical landscape. He prepared numerous musical
editions, and college choruses still program "Riu riu chiu" (a Spanish
Renaissance carol) at Christmastime, complete with the tambourine
parts that Noah wrote in for people who didn't know how to impro-
vise. In less specific ways, the Pro Musica ethos has spread far and
wide. Currently active ensembles like the Waverly Consort in New
York, the Boston Camerata, and the London Early Music Group are
directed by musicians who developed in or near Greenberg's orbit. In
some ways, too, the success of such showman-oriented European

---

combinations of voices and instruments in his *Syntagma musicum.* But Pro Musica's approach to scoring, we see now in retrospect, owed a lot to the American
big band era. Ferde Grofé and Fletcher Henderson had their indirect hand, too, in
the New York Pro Musica's sound.

groups as the late David Munrow's Early Music Consort of London or the Vienna-based Clemencic Consort was prefigured and prepared for by the Greenberg *maniera*.

Still, the best way to keep Noah Greenberg's spirit alive may have little to do with a specific style of concertizing. Should Renaissance concerts be happy and extroverted, or should they be sober and scholarly? It's a false quarrel, since the repertoires themselves are so varied and so inclusive of myriad spiritual states: any number of different programming approaches and style options can have their own truth and their own "authenticity."* To stay faithful to the Greenberg heritage, we need to seek out new things among the old works, to try out new ways of approaching the music, and to imagine ourselves farther and deeper than ever before into the psychic center of the musical past. The externals of presentation will follow along later, and naturally, if the musical instincts are good and true.

I was a beginning lutenist; a year earlier, a New York Pro Musica concert in Providence, Rhode Island, had blown my mind and had made me, a college undergraduate, decide that early music was what I wanted to do. Now the ensemble was back in town and Noah Greenberg was giving me an afternoon of his time, freely sharing with a young man he barely knew his thoughts on music, career, and the meaning of life.

As we walked up College Hill toward the Brown campus, after a dense discussion on the relative merits of Elizabethan and Italian lute repertoires, Greenberg began to turn philosophical. "If I believed in an afterlife," he said, "I think I would have stayed on as a labor organizer. But this life in the here and now is the one we have to deal with. So I've decided to spend my time creating beautiful music."

Three years later Noah disappeared from the only plane of exis-

---

* Of course, we have learned more about historical performance practice since the 1950s. Some things that were accepted as lively and imaginative reconstruction even a few years ago (example: adding percussion parts to music for the Mass) were probably never done in the very old days. Still, much of the debate about historical practice has more to do with twentieth-century trends than some people care to admit.

tence in which he really believed and trusted. Like a true Renaissance man, he had chosen to realize himself in the fragile, fleeting moment of sensory pleasure. I do not know if his metaphysics were good or bad; but I am certain that he was one extraordinary human being. May his spirit live on in all of us who cherish the songs of our fathers and their fathers before us!

VI

Thomas Binkley

*J*UST a few years after the peak of Pro Musica's popularity, in the mid-1960s, news began to reach the American shores, via recordings, of a radically "different" Medieval-Renaissance ensemble. The records, magnificently produced by Wolf Ericson, appeared on the Telefunken label in the series Das alte Werk. There were just four regular members of this group, which bore the forbidding moniker "Studio der Fruehen Musik"; despite the German title, three-quarters of the members' names were Anglo-Saxon: Binkley, Jones, and Rogers. Only Andrea von Ramm's surname seemed to justify a priori the "München" that appeared after the group's title; and the unclassifiable Andrea, we were to find out later, was born in Estonia.

The recordings sent shock waves throughout the American early music community. Instrumentation was sparse — had to be, with only two regular players on the roster — and the playing in those first recordings seemed sometimes unduly peckish and choppy. The most unsettling thing, though, was the singing. Sacrilege! The voices were an affront to everything considered good and holy in conservatories and community music schools. These singers would not be hired to sing *Messiah* in Peoria or Laramie or New York City. Here was light, articulate voice production, barely removed at times from speech itself. Instead of the heavy-cream, vibrato-laden, all-systems-are-go approach synonymous with "serious" music in the mid-twentieth-century canon of vocal art, Andrea von Ramm and Nigel Rogers opted for other values. Their singing contained little or no vibrato, was never pushed for volume's sake, and utilized the various registers of the voice individually, as the musical contexts shifted around. Von Ramm's unique and inimitable sound (her natural voice lies in the tenor range, and she has cultivated falsetto singing much as a countertenor would) made Studio's approach more controversial still. After all, it was widely assumed (still is in some circles) that singing is singing.* The way it's done today in opera and oratorio is the best way, and deviations from that norm must be a sign of ineptitude. The Studio was deviant! Cries of "amateurism" were rampant in the land.

Undeterred (nay, encouraged) by all the controversy, Studio continued to tour and perform extensively. Nigel Rogers left early on for a brilliant solo career; the core group of von Ramm, Binkley, and Sterling Jones added first tenor Willard Cobb and then countertenor Richard Levitt ("they take the male singer out of a trunk just before each concert," said one observer, somewhat unfairly, during the retiring Cobb's stint with the ensemble).

Studio's recordings were generally made with the help of additional guest performers. But only four musicians did the concert tours. Performing from memory, intensely concentrated, with von Ramm's dynamic stage presence and extraordinary three-octave vocal range, driven forward by Binkley's restless, relentless curiosity, the ensemble made an enormous impact on its audiences.

Studio's numerous recordings provide a reasonably fair overview of the group's artistic development. In the early days, the emphasis was on lightweight anthology programs, with a smattering of this and that: fifteenth-century Burgundian chansons, Italian *frottole* from

---

* I last heard the formulation "singing is singing" very recently, in a graduate seminar meeting on the English madrigal. The superbly intelligent scholar of Renaissance music who thus expressed himself is not alone in thinking that voice production and color are basically the same no matter what kind of music you want to sing. The easiest way to refute that idea is to imagine Elisabeth Schwarzkopf tremulating "Empty Bed Blues" — or Bessie Smith ripping into "Die Forelle."

the early sixteenth century, Spanish miniatures, and so forth. The practice of mixing many styles and periods in an early music recital had been the norm since the Dolmetsch days, and in fact still prevails in many places. The difference between Studio's smorgasbord and the others' lay in Studio's very unusual and accomplished performance style.

Gradually, however, the group began performing fewer of the Renaissance entertainment pieces that had been a large part of its early repertoire ("music for tired businessmen" was what Binkley called that kind of programming). Binkley always had been interested in Medieval monody, and Studio had begun staking out claims in that territory with a mid-1960s recording of songs from the *Carmina Burana* manuscript.* And it was in the Medieval repertoires that Studio was to make its biggest and most lasting contribution.

Now the revival of Baroque music (which we will be discussing in later chapters) is based in large part on rather precise performing treatises from the seventeenth and eighteenth centuries; treatises that were known about but that had been neglected by performers until recent years. The guidelines for interpreting Medieval music are much less clear; the very notation of early Medieval music is so

---

* The term "monody" in the context of Medieval music refers to poetry accompanied by one notated melodic line. About three hundred monodic songs survive in Old Provençal; about two thousand in Old French; and thousands more in twelfth- and thirteenth-century Latin manuscripts. A tradition of German monodic singing survived well into the sixteenth century (remember Wagner's *Die Meistersinger?*). Most Western art music since the early Middle Ages has been polyphonic in nature, combining two or more musical lines simultaneously.

Thanks to German composer Carl Orff, one corner of the monodic repertoire has intruded into the general consciousness. Orff fashioned a spectacular oratorio-cum-ballet around some twelfth-century Latin and German poems composed by students and clerics and preserved in a Bavarian monastery. The *Carmina Burana* poems, set to (nonmonodic) music for huge orchestra and chorus by Orff, have achieved immense popularity in the twentieth century. It is considered heretical in early music circles to admire Orff's musical settings: one really *ought* to prefer the melodies, tenuously preserved in the original manuscript. Binkley, and later René Clemencic, reconstructed some of the *Carmina Burana* tunes according to their own lights; the rollicking Orff oratorio now has some competition from the early instrument camp.

sketchy that we can never have a very precise idea of how those works were performed long ago.

You have to intuit and hypothesize about one kind of music from the past. But in Medieval music, especially, there is a very large component of educated guesswork. A thirteenth-century troubadour song will be notated (if indeed there is a melody at all to accompany the poem) with only a single line of music: no accompaniment, no polyphony, no precise indication of rhythm. From this very minimal record the modern-day interpreter must somehow evolve a complete performance. The cautious approach generally favored until Binkley's arrival on the scene pretended that Medieval notation was like modern "classical" notation: the composer was assumed to have set down on paper the sounds he wanted to hear.

Binkley and Studio assumed that the notation of Medieval monody, like the lead-sheets used by jazz and pop musicians of today, represented only a sketch or a shorthand record of the actual musical sounds, and that it was desirable and necessary to flesh out the written page with embellishments, accompaniments, and various enrichments which Medieval performers (like jazz musicians) never wrote down.

Binkley extended the time-scale of the Medieval songs. He routinely gave most of the original text. This would seem to be the most normal approach, but many performances of Medieval monody present only one or two strophes of a long poem; modern performers are too often unacquainted with the literary and linguistic side of Medieval music, and perhaps scared as well of boring their audiences. Binkley wasn't scared. He abjured the Medieval-music-as-aperitif approach and gave entire recitals of monody, seven or eight strophes per poem, and with elaborate instrumental accompaniments surrounding those strophes. Here was a source of even greater controversy: the poetry itself was a faithful representation of the old sources, but the accompaniments were the product of Binkley's imagination.

And what accompaniments! Studio was determined to fill in the sounds it believed the manuscripts had omitted. Middle Eastern ouds and darbouks began sharing onstage space with the organetto and the vielle. The preludes and interludes devised by Studio often had a decidedly Oriental flavor, both in their methods of musical construction and in the styles of ornamentation and articulation the instrumentalists came to adapt. These newly conceived instrumental passages often took up as much or more performing time as the notated vocal music they surrounded.

Indeed, some of Studio's most intense and moving performances were constructed almost out of thin air. I remember hearing a twelfth-century "Planctus," or lamentation piece, by the famed Peter Abelard performed by Studio in the little chapel at Les Baux-de-Provence in the mid-1970s. Abelard's work, as performed that day by the four musicians of the Studio, lasted around twenty minutes, and included elaborate transformations of the melodic material, frequent tempo shifts, unusual rhythmic patterns from a Moroccan tambourine, and imaginative, eloquent responses to the singers from Sterling Jones's vielle. The audience crowded into the tiny chapel was visibly enthralled.

Yet many compromises had been made en route to achieving that miraculous moment in Les Baux. Abelard's music (as Binkley readily admitted in a post-concert chat) had been written for female voices, for the women of the convent headed by his beloved Héloïse. Adding instrumental parts to the vocal lines in this particular case was hard to justify on historical grounds. And even the contours of the singing parts were hard to determine; Abelard's music was notated in neumes, a system that records musical gestures but not exact pitches. Almost everything Studio had done was open to question. The only verifiable "facts" were two: the Latin poem, and Studio's magnificent performance.

When Studio ventured into the later Middle Ages, its efforts remained controversial. The music of the fourteenth century is much less ambiguous in its notation than that of the twelfth; pitches and rhythms are clearly indicated. Here Binkley challenged not the symbols themselves, but our conventional ways of understanding them. For example: it is a *sine qua non* of the way we make music nowadays that performers must try to play together. An orchestra or string quartet that fails to achieve simultaneity of ensemble, with precisely calculated attacks and releases, is unlikely to win raves from the critics, and for good reason. The ways of expressing musical thought that underlie our Western system demand careful coordination on the musicians' part. You can't hope to understand what is going on in a Bach fugue or a Mozart aria if the different polyphonic strands are not lined up together.

Yet on more than a few Studio recordings, you will hear deliberate attempts among the performers *not* to stay together, except at key structural points: beginnings, ends, and important cadences. Listen to Studio performing Guillaume de Machaut: each musical line seeks out its own flow, its own gesture. We know that Medieval polyphony was composed one line at a time; why not try to perform it in a way that reflects that linearity? By daring to ask such probing questions, the Studio managed to come up with unusual interpretations. And when their experimentation bore fruitful results, listeners were able to partake in some extraordinary and powerful musical experiences.

Nowhere in the early music scene is the tug-of-war between the scientific and the intuitive more clearly delineated. Like politicians, early music practitioners often say one thing and do another; the ideology of the "authentic" performance is constantly at odds with the concrete problems of making old music heard now. Thomas Binkley is the son of a famous American historian, and a teacher himself (at the Schola Cantorum of Basel and later at the University of Indiana). His intensely felt loyalty to the "objective" methods of modern scholarship (see our later discussion of musicology as a discipline in Chapter XIV) have made him loath to admit that his approach to Medieval music owed so very much to personal intuition.

Scholarship was, in fact, an important component of Studio's work. Binkley's knowledge of original sources was extensive, and his background in the social and cultural history of the Middle Ages superior by far to the average performer's. He replied to accusations that Studio's Medieval performances were overelaborated and largely fictitious with a torrent of verbal arguments, including theories about regional performing styles and the usefulness of disciplined performance practice within arbitrarily chosen conventions. He was a nervous explainer.

Studio had to defend its positions on two fronts: the scholars found them too wild and freaky. But at the other pole, a whole slew of semiprofessional noodlers and doodlers copied some superficial aspects of Binkley's performance style, creating weird *salades composées* of Bernard de Ventadorn and Ravi Shankar.

The Studio's explanations went down the tubes, not because their performances were bad but because their methods of exegesis were flawed. They tried to justify their choices on scientific grounds, when in fact they were performing a leap of faith every time they sat down to play together. When Studio borrowed performance techniques from Arabic music or flamenco singing or Balkan folk music, they were just guessing. The guesswork was brilliant, educated, and often plausible, but it could not be proved by the scholarly method. Besides their special qualities of intellectual resourcefulness, Studio supplied in ample measure the other necessaries of good practice in most any musical style, including lots of brio and showmanship.

Above all, Binkley and his colleagues were willing to invent the music they played — and I say this without the slightest intention of mockery. Like a good jazz player, the performer of Medieval monody has to bring a very large measure of him- or herself to a performance. If you cannot or will not rethink a troubadour or trouvère song from the inside out, your modern-day performance is probably going to fall flat.

Right or wrong about their specific decisions, Studio showed us that one has to take risks to make very old music come alive. They established once and for all that Medieval song cannot be done like Schubert or even Dowland. Conventional, conservatory-style singing was revealed to be woefully inadequate to the demands of very old repertoire. And the overly timid approach to performing early Medieval works was seen to be a way of avoiding the center of that music, rather than coming to grips with it.

Coming to grips was the very essence of what Studio did. Binkley wrestled with Peter Abelard like Jacob with the angel. You could hear the bones cracking for miles around, but at least you were aware that *something* was going on. The surest way to kill the great music of the past is through blandness and timid hesitancy. Better to get bruised by struggling with an angel than to sit at home contemplating the head of a pin.

VII

Baroque Renewal

*T*HE impresario was perplexed. "Why won't the Conservatory hire them to give a master class? After all, I'm bringing them to town for a concert at the school's own recital hall. And the concert is sold out!"

The unhappy concert manager, himself an early music fan, could not understand why his featured artists, the magnificent Kuijken brothers, were not being invited to give their master class at a major institution of musical education. Was not this school committed to high artistic standards? Were not the Kuijkens — gambist Wieland, violinist Sigiswald, and flautist Bart — acknowledged masters of their instruments, and pioneers of Baroque performance practice?* It was hard for the kindly and generous manager to realize that his musicians were probably being refused a forum precisely because of their superb and therefore dangerous achievement. The Kuijkens' ways were different, and in all likelihood a threat to the local music teachers. Sigiswald and Bart played well-known instruments, but they played them in unconventional ways. Too risky for a conservative music school!

* For further discussion of the Kuijkens see Chapter IX ; see also the Photograph Section.

The hardest changes to accept are the ones that occur close to home. Our worst enemies are often people like ourselves. We fear the Russians more than the Chinese; we have more trouble getting along with our parents than with our friends; and it takes four sopranos to change a light bulb (one to insert the new bulb and three others to pull away the chair she is standing on).

Given these unfortunate tendencies of human nature, the controversies over Baroque string playing should have come as no surprise. The recorder and the rebec, the gamba and the crwth, are not familiar members of the symphony orchestra. Musicians who revived and performed on such obsolete instruments are easily regarded as amiable eccentrics.

But beware of tampering with things familiar! It may be relatively unthreatening to exhume trottos and saltarellos of the fourteenth century with vielles and organettos; only a handful of devotees have any notion of that repertoire to begin with. When you start performing Bach and Vivaldi and Mozart in the "early music" way — well, that is another can of catgut altogether. To play the familiar violin and cello with the unfamiliar techniques of the eighteenth century is to invite controversy and anger. We think we already know what the correct way of performing Bach or Vivaldi or Mozart should be.

Beware the Baroque violinist with her curved bow, her gut strings, her peculiar thin outlandish too soft not rich enough not loud enough not wobbly enough not exciting enough above all not familiar enough sound. She will drive you crazy with too-short phrases and her infuriating habit of making a swell on every long note! She will corrupt the youth and give them wrong ideas of what great music is supposed to sound like! She will tamper with our most precious cultural relics; she will make them unfamiliar again! And by making those relics unfamiliar, she will rob them of their quasi-liturgical power. I told you those damn fiddle players were a bunch of atheists!

No such imprecations surrounded the revival of Medieval and Renaissance music: those centuries were just too far away to count that much. The challenge to established ways of performing late Baroque and pre-classical music was by far the most controversial part of the whole early music movement. The finest Baroque string players and the most skilled ensembles have had to impose their renewed vision of the music in the face of angry opposition, sometimes from critics and the public at large, often from musician colleagues. The late-Baroque light bulbs are getting changed, but many people have done all they could to pull the chair away.

What were the things that made the conservatory teachers so hostile?

Lots of things, including some of the most basic precepts of interpretive style as taught in the nineteenth century and after. Every budding pianist and violinist and singer is taught nowadays to make very long musical phrases, with the notes closely linked in a long line. The young music student begins by playing everything as connected ("legato") as possible. Afterward, she or he learns about other kinds of articulation, but the basic goal is still to make a long and connected line.

The Romantic music of Brahms and Verdi is admirably served by this approach; the expansive, surging phrases of the nineteenth-century masters demand from the performers the grand gesture and the singing sostenuto. And everyone assumed that earlier music, too, ought to be performed in the same way.

You cannot, of course, perform Bach well without knowing how to make the lines "sing": but how different are the phrasing conventions of the eighteenth century! Look closely at the curved bow of the Baroque violin and you will see a tool for shaping lithe, supple groups of notes. The modern, convex bow is ideally suited to the connected, legato style; the Baroque bow, in contrast, encourages a lighter, more "speaking" approach.

The convex form of the modern bow makes it easy to keep each note consistent in intensity from the beginning of the attack to the end. The arched bow of the Baroque tends to draw the sound out in the middle of each note: a pitch will tend to begin softly, swell toward the center, and taper off toward the end.

Contemplate the other parts of the Baroque fiddle, and see how they, too, tend to change the expressive content of a performance. The neck is shorter, the interior barring different on a Baroque instrument. The gut strings are typically tuned to a lower pitch standard than are a modern instrument's. The Baroque violin can be put through many virtuoso paces: but it is still a quieter, more intimate kind of animal than its modern descendant.

The morphology of a musical instrument, the way it is put together by its maker, has a great deal to do with what listeners want to hear. Technique does not exist in a spiritual vacuum. If a rock guitarist can easily purchase a million-megawatt amp with which to deafen his audience (and himself), that is because many fans today enjoy contemplating art at the threshold of pain.

Conversely, if the Baroque violin is more discreet, more subtle than its modern counterpart, that is because finesse and discretion were important aesthetic goals two centuries ago, just as power and physical intensity are expressive aims today. The Baroque violin was admirably adapted to the music it was called on to play.

Reading the old how-to-do-it books for the budding violinists of the Baroque era tends to confirm this insight. The way an instrument is put together and the way it should be played are closely interrelated! The Baroque bow tends to make a lozenge-shaped note, with a swell in the middle; lo and behold, the old tutorials encourage the player to cultivate this natural tendency for its expressive effect. The old curved bow is wonderfully suited for rapid, subtle changes of nuance within a phrase; and the treatises tell the young player to make his musical line correspond to the rise and fall of human speech. The innards of a Baroque violin produce many rich and beautifully colored overtones; when you hear the Bach solo suites on such an instrument, the web of sound is sustained by the resonances coming from within the fiddle. The same works performed on a modern violin seem strained and unnatural in comparison. The instrument, the technique of playing, and the expressive aims of the music form a closely linked and indissociable whole.

Yet the resistance to these renewed perceptions of Baroque music was strong. People had enjoyed hearing their Bach done up the modern way. They liked the higher pitch, the loud and powerful sound of today's stringed instruments. They went for the thrilling thrust and swoop of the modern orchestra. "If Bach had known about these wonderful instruments, he would surely have made use of them," exclaimed the anxious defenders of grand pianos, renecked Strads, and Wagner tubas.

Gradually, though, our ears have become accustomed to the sounds of Baroque instruments. We can now hear what they have to say to us about the great music of the seventeenth and eighteenth centuries without groping for the security blanket of nineteenth-century conventions. By coming closer to the music of the past, we can take even greater pleasure than before in some very great expressions of the human spirit. The crazy geniuses who first attempted, nearly a century ago, to make the old instruments speak again, have ultimately wrought a miracle of regeneration and renewal. Enduring the wheezes and squeaks of the first, experimental years, persisting in the face of hostile critics and mistrustful colleagues, the pioneers of the distant past (and their successors) have won through to new skills and to new insights. "If the fool would persist in his folly he would become wise," wrote William Blake. And that is exactly what has happened.

VIII

The Harnoncourts & Concentus Musicus

IT took a while for the first tentative plantings of renewal to bear fruit. Arnold Dolmetsch was playing Baroque violin in the twenties, but the audible results were probably less than completely satisfying in terms of finish and accuracy. In this country, the courageous Sol Babitz experimented with Baroque violin techniques back in the fifties; his ideas seemed outlandish to many at the time, but most of his positions have since been vindicated. Still, it was not until 1960 or thereabouts that the world was to hear a fully professional chamber orchestra that used period instruments and period techniques as a matter of course.

Nikolaus Harnoncourt (b. 1929) began his career as an orchestral cellist; his wife, Alice, trained with the best teachers of modern violin. And they brought to their ensemble, the Vienna-based Concentus Musicus, a strong and sure musical sense to supplement their wide-ranging intellectual curiosity. The Concentus is mainly known nowadays for its work in seventeenth- and eighteenth-century music — but in the early years, the group performed and recorded extensively the Medieval and Renaissance repertoire as well. From the very start, the public knew it had discovered something very special. Here was an ensemble that actively sought out the unusual and the untried.

[51]

Beyond that, here were musicians capable of playing the works they had turned up with a high degree of polish and panache. A page had been turned: early repertoire on authentic instruments did not *have* to be performed with inadequate technique.

The core group of Concentus played all kinds of historical stringed instruments: violas da gamba and vielles figured prominently in the ensemble's early history. The Concentus's initial success came in 1962, with a recording of Bach's concertos played on period instruments; from then on Baroque music was the ensemble's main preoccupation. The instrumental timbres of those Bach recordings from the sixties now seem, a generation later, surprisingly Romantic and "Viennese"; but at the time they appeared radically, violently different.

It was obvious from the beginning that these musicians had some strong ideas about how to proceed. The Baroque strings and winds had their characteristic sounds; equally controversial was Nikolaus Harnoncourt's approach to rhythmic articulation. The skilled performer of Romantic music learns to make a smooth line and to avoid strong, systematic acccents. Harnoncourt pointed out that the older way of doing things made an important aural distinction among the beats in a measure. In a cycle of four beats, "one" was the most important, "three" was next in intensity, "two" was a weak beat, and "four" was the weakest of all. These are rules that children learn as beginning music students, and that they spend years trying to unlearn at conservatory. But for some parts at least of the Baroque repertoire, they were important precepts. In the seventeenth-century music of Jean-Baptiste Lully, for example, you are supposed to hear the beginning of each measure; careful descriptions from the period leave little doubt on that score. At Versailles all the "vingt-quatre violons" played with the same accented bowstroke as each new measure came around, and Lully himself beat time on the floor with a stick. The poor man eventually punctured his foot in an excess of directorial enthusiasm; he died of the ensuing infection. None of our "authentic" Baroque ensembles has yet tried to replicate this particular detail of French performance practice.

But several of them have done their best to recreate the rhythmic feeling (or feelings) of that period — and here was Concentus, heretically proposing *its* solution. *Thump* went the downbeats, as regular and inevitable as the judge's gavel in small claims court. Perhaps Harnoncourt, in his commendable desire to unglue one beat from the next, went a little too far. Some of the Concentus performances seemed too dogmatic, too systematized, to make entire musical sense.

Some, but not all. For Harnoncourt, his wife, and his associates are extraordinary and sensitive players. On a good day, they make the music leap and spin. Bass lines are superbly clean and full of life (cellist Harnoncourt is an excellent continuist); inner voices are finely delineated; and the melodic parts are chiseled and shaped in a way that blends careful historical research with a healthy measure of Central European cantabile.

By showing what first-rate orchestral players could do on early instruments, Concentus helped destroy the myth that one performed older music because of some underlying personal handicap or weakness. (The core group of Concentus had been recruited from musicians of the Vienna Symphony Orchestra; for years, you could glimpse Harnoncourt in that cello section during the traditional New Year's Day telecast of Strauss waltzes.) The playing of violinist Alice Harnoncourt, oboist Jürg Schaeftlein, and flautist Leopold Stasny is exemplary in polish and fluency. When bassoonist Milan Turkovic unleashes the solo part of a Vivaldi concerto, the concert space overflows with bass-clef burbles, like the water-filled cellar in the famous Disney cartoon of *The Sorcerer's Apprentice*. To be sure, critics complained at the beginning that Concentus couldn't play the instruments. The critics were talking through their hats; this is a very high-powered group.

Harnoncourt and Concentus began an extensive recording program of major works from the seventeenth and eighteenth centuries: Monteverdi operas, Bach's major instrumental and choral works (including a still-incomplete series of all the cantatas). Much of this large-scale repertoire centered around the human voice, and here Harnoncourt's instincts were less sure than when he was dealing with instruments. Some of the soloists he engaged for his operatic productions were too attached to their plummy wobbles to blend well with the orchestral sonorities. Nonetheless, some of the finest moments in Concentus's discography involve the collaboration of singers and players. The wonderful taste and control of Max von Egmond, the magnificent text declamation of Kurt Equiluz, add immeasurably to Concentus's performances of Bach passions and Bach cantatas.

Isolation from peers is a problem in the early music world. Some specialist performers even take pride in the distance they put between themselves and every other kind of musical activity. Harnoncourt has gone far in the other direction. His desire to touch many people is evident in the "standard" repertoire he frequently directs. That same urge has perhaps inspired his ambitious, large-scale modern productions of Baroque opera. Stage director Jean-Pierre Ponelle is no historian of theater, and the Monteverdi operas he undertook with Harnoncourt at Zurich in the seventies contained many frankly contemporary elements. The film they made of Monteverdi's *Orfeo* has both weaknesses and strengths: the cliché-ridden crowd movements and the sometimes unstylish singing are offset by an unforgettable, chilling decor for the underworld scenes, and the vital, incisive playing from the orchestra pit (which contained both Concentus regulars and members of the Zurich opera orchestra).

Missionarylike, Harnoncourt has tried to bring his insights into early music performance to the modern orchestral milieu. Some of the musicians in the Zurich productions of Monteverdi were modern-instrument players retrained for the occasion. And recently, Harnoncourt has been guest-conducting some large modern orchestras (such as the Amsterdam Concertgebouw) in performances of Mozart. Unlike Frans Brüggen, whose Orchestra of the Eighteenth Century is made up of early music specialists, Harnoncourt has decided to expend considerable time and effort with "modern" players. And he has in fact managed to obtain some extraordinary results. The Mozart performances of Harnoncourt's "modern orchestra" period have been among the most convincing of his entire career. The perfumed aesthete we often seem to perceive in conventional Mozart playing has been replaced by someone else! Harnoncourt's Mozart is dynamic, vigorous, a man full of tempestuous energy, a creature of the theater from first to last. We have caught a glimpse of Mozart the Romantic, thanks, ironically, to someone who came from much earlier music. It took the unhackneyed perspective of an early music "outsider" to make us hear the strength and modernity of music sometimes perceived to be frilly, decorative, and *ancien régime.*

The sheer vastness of Harnoncourt's life project, the size of Concentus's discography, the continuing evolution of these musicians — all these things make it hard to summarize their contribution in a few lines of text. One can, of course, quibble with some of their decisions and stylistic options. One can always oppose another sensibility, another way of doing things, to theirs — even within the framework of the historicist, early instrument approach. What lies by now beyond challenge is the permanent change these people have brought about in our musical life. The early music world has always had to defend itself against accusations of amateurism. Frequently, there was some truth in the charges: many performers at the movement's inception had nimbler intellects than they did fingers.

Concentus set new standards for professional performance on old instruments. They stood, and stand, as a living rebuke to those who proclaimed it impossible to play early instruments really well. They gave us living actualizations of many masterpieces — works whose true content had been partially obscured by misunderstanding and lazy habit.

And they gave a still younger generation a model to emulate, a standard to surpass if possible. Harnoncourt was and is a risk-taker. When some current specialist magazines accuse him of "overinterpretation," they are throwing pebbles at a giant. In this decade, one current of early music fashion encourages presenting a seamless, nearly decisionless surface of sound to the listening public. Harnoncourt's way has been the more daring and, I think, the more profoundly "authentic." His performances have a center, a strong point of view. We will be arguing for years over their specifics, but not about their underlying spirit.

IX

The Kuijkens

"HAVE you ever heard anything like it?" My questioner, a programmer for France Musique, the classical music radio station in Paris, was talking about a newly arrived recording. "They don't play this music the way people are used to hearing it. Not at all. If we air this, we're going to get some more angry mail.

"Anyway, they're not even French. We should give priority to our own, native performers in this repertoire, don't you agree?"

I had a hard time agreeing, for two reasons. First, I was no Frenchman myself, and my presence at the station was itself cause for suspicion among the chauvinistically inclined. Second, and more important, the recording in question was superb, a stunning document. That performance of Couperin by a Belgian-Dutch consortium headed by the Kuijken brothers was the very best thing of its kind I had ever come across. In my opinion the recording (which eventually did get on the air, and many times) should have been distributed at every corner bakery in France, as a bonus giveaway. Buy three croissants, and you get early instrument Couperin for free! This would have assured wide popular acceptance of some delicious but strangely unappreciated aspects of French civilization. For French music (especially the older branches) was a lot like New

England weather. It was a favorite subject of conversation, but nobody ever seemed to do very much about it.

In any case, no one seemed to do very much about it in France itself, where attempts to perform the music of Jean-Philippe Rameau, Jean-Baptiste Lully, François Couperin, and other French masters of the Baroque usually failed to arouse much enthusiasm. Despite the ritual nods toward their glorious past, neither the French public nor the professonal musician caste seemed to have much real flair or passion for their uniquely fascinating heritage. With only a few exceptions (such as the lively opera productions directed by Jean-Claude Malgoire, a trailblazing entrepreneur) the French musician who performed repertoire earlier than Berlioz did so with a certain grim resignation. "Please, gentlemen," said one eminent conductor to his orchestra as he rehearsed an opera by André Campra (1660–1744). "Try to play together. The music is bad enough as it is."

The French players had lost the key to their own past. And who else was going to unlock those treasure chests? For the music of France is uniquely culture-bound; in no other part of Europe are style and substance so intimately one. You can perform Vivaldi with kazoos or Hawaiian guitars, and something of the composer's intentions will still come across. But unless the manner and the gesture are just exactly right, the music of Lully or Rameau will sound drab and unconvincing. To excel in French music, you must get every detail just right; all the elements of style must be in place, or you will fall flat, like the hostess who serves her guests Coca-Cola with the quiche.

To play French music well, you must have some feeling for or empathy with French culture in general. And you must be patient, hard-working, and willing to take risks. While everyone in France fulfills the first condition, only a few French people involved in the arts pass muster for all the others. And so it came to pass that we first began hearing superb performances of French Baroque music from musicians with odd names: not Dupont and Dubois, as you might expect, but Kohnen, Rubinlicht, Kuijken. From Belgians!

Like most of their Belgian compatriots, the members of the Alarius ensemble — violinists Janine Rubinlicht and Sigiswald Kuijken, harpsichordist Robert Kohnen, and gambist Wieland Kuijken — were bilingual and bicultural. Had the Kuijkens been Dutch or German by birth, they might have learned English as a second language, but since they grew up near Brussels, they assimilated French along with their native Flemish. And their way with French music has a lot to do, I am sure, with the unique cultural situation of the Flemings. From Josquin des Prez to César Franck, much of the richest vein in Gallic music making has been mined north of Paris. The Kuijkens and their colleagues continue a long Low Countries tradition of bringing French music back to the French.

Of course, the Kuijkens and their circle play more than French repertoire. The old Alarius ensemble, the current Kuijken ensemble, and Sigiswald's orchestra, La Petite Bande, made up of the best Baroque players in Belgium and the Netherlands, regularly perform Baroque and pre-classical works from all European repertoires. Sigiswald's recordings of the Bach violin and harpsichord sonatas (with Gustav Leonhardt) are justly famous. And flautist Bart can make Georg Philipp Telemann's solo fantasias sound like major works, so subtly inflected is his playing of them.

Something even more extraordinary happens, however, when gambist Wieland sits down to play works of *le grand siècle*. The suites of Versailles court composer Marin Marais reveal themselves to the fullest in Wieland's hands. All the pomp, all the haughty pride of the French courtier emerge from the rapid bowstrokes and the sharp, angular rhythms. More than that, though: Wieland's viola da gamba sings of joy, of tender affection, of longing, and of the fear of death. Behind the powdered wigs and the perfumed lace we can perceive another man's soul. Is it the composer's music that moves us so? The expressive power of the viola da gamba? The incredible poetry and refinement of Wieland's playing? It's all of those things in combination: for a few minutes we have transcended all issues of style, technique, and historicity to confront the living center of Music itself.

The Kuijken brothers did not arrive on Parnassus unassisted. The original Alarius ensemble was an intergenerational collaboration; Rubinlicht and Kohnen served as mentors to the younger Sigiswald and Wieland. On the first Alarius recordings from the 1960s, you can hear fine and sensitive playing of Baroque works — but the style of bowing and the articulation still owe a lot to modern orchestral practice. Through study, trial, and error the Belgian string players eventually developed a style of playing even more radical than the one favored by Harnoncourt's Concentus Musicus. The Romantic roots were still evident in Alice Harnoncourt's solo playing with Concentus; the on-the-string legato and continuous vibrato she favored were rejected by the Brussels players. Many crisp, short bow-strokes alternated with the longer ones. (Watching Janine Rubinlicht give a downbeat is like being admitted to Vulcan's workshop as the god prepares to strike a hammer blow.) Vibrato was almost totally suppressed; it reappeared as an occasional ornament on longer notes. Air and light flooded the interstices of each musical phrase.

The style of string playing evolved by the Brussels players (and their colleagues in Amsterdam, including Lucy van Dael and Anner Bylsma) has been widely admired and emulated in other parts of the world. To a young gambist or Baroque violinist, being accepted for study with a Kuijken is the equivalent of getting into Harvard or MIT. The mass media, as usual, have been the last to catch on; only a season or two ago *The New York Times* critic wondered in print who Wieland Kuijken was.

Indeed, until very recently the Kuijkens had an off-again on-again relationship with the musical establishment of their own country. "What did you say their names were?" asked the artistic director of Belgium's largest opera house when he was approached about hiring them for a Baroque opera production. And the head of a large Flemish conservatory where Wieland was giving lessons asked a member of the violin faculty if that gamba teacher people were talking about was really any good! The violinist in question, a member of La Petite Bande, answered "Yes," and walked away, shaking his head.

The self-important poobahs of our cultural establishment are still asleep at the wheel in most other ways concerning early music. But not so the public. The Kuijken brothers, offering a late-night performance of six Haydn trios, filled a Utrecht church to capacity during the 1983 early music festival: the musicians' concentration on and involvement with the music were matched at every step by the public's, despite the ungodly late hour and the uncompromising program. And when Wieland Kuijken performed Marin Marais's "Le tombeau de Monsieur Blancrocher" in Boston a few seasons ago, I saw members of the audience moved to tears by his playing.

As the Kuijken brothers mature and evolve, the differences among them become more apparent. Wieland and Bart seem happy and fulfilled as instrumental practitioners; the gamba and the transverse flute, and the repertoires closely linked with those instruments, are their finite means for achieving infinite ends.

Brother Sigiswald, who seems to have the most thorny and Faustian personality of the three, has been turning more and more to conducting La Petite Bande; we have been hearing him as director of opera by Handel and oratorio by Haydn (and he once confided to me that he had a secret ambition to perform Brahms).

Sigiswald Kuijken is not the only early music specialist to lust in his heart for Romantic music — see also our discussion of Harnoncourt and Brüggen as Mozarteans. We now have early instrument performances of Schubert and Beethoven, and we may yet get to hear the Brahms symphonies done with natural horns and trumpets. (There are also critics crying out for more authentic performances of Gershwin; the orchestrations of his symphonic works have apparently been considerably mucked up over the years. Early music, as we have said already, is only secondarily a given body of repertoire. It is first and foremost a collective frame of mind among a community of modern-day people.)

The Kuijkens (like many of the musicians in their circle) are still young, and still likely to offer us many new surprises and insights. The guidebooks say Belgium is a sleepy country — but what do official guides know about living reality? Trust that Baedeker (and this one, too!) no more than the next. Better to seek out for yourself, as the Kuijkens have done, the true secrets of art, the precious, hidden dwelling place of the Muse.

X

Frans Brüggen

O_F all the melody instruments, the most important during the seventeenth and eighteenth centuries was unquestionably the violin; the transverse flute trailed forlornly at a distant second place. Yet the first modern superstar to emerge from the early music ranks was neither a violinist nor (primarily) a traverso player. His instrument was the one favored by countless thousands of early music enthusiasts — the recorder. He was a Dutchman named Frans Brüggen (b. 1934).

His enormous public success surpassed anything previously conferred on an early instrument specialist (except perhaps for harpsichordist Wanda Landowska two generations earlier). Brüggen's public included, but went far beyond, the relatively restrained coterie of the early music faithful. No one ever threatened to make Gustav Leonhardt or Sigiswald Kuijken into a matinee idol; but around 1968 Telefunken, which was releasing solo recitals by Brüggen on a regular basis, began packaging a poster-size photograph of their star with some of his albums. The handsome virtuoso, heavy-lidded and weary of this mortal frame, gazed out from the photo, past the solicitations of his adoring fans, toward some profound and mysteriously burdensome Unknown. Large numbers of artistic and sensitive young ladies affixed the poster to their bedroom walls.*

* See the Photograph Section for pictures of Brüggen.

The recorder was one of the first obsolete instruments to be revived in modern times. This unpromising stick of wood has also been known as the *blockflöte, flûte à bec,* or occasionally just plain flute. It has shared a long history with its sister instrument, the transverse flute (also known as the *flauto traverso, flûte allemande,* German flute, or occasionally just plain flute). But the transverse flute, despite numerous transformations of its manufacture across the centuries (or rather because of them), never went out of style. The modern orchestral flute, many-keyed and silver-bright, descends in a straight line from the wooden *traversi* of earlier centuries.

The recorder has no comparable place in modern concert life. Its decline and fall had to do perhaps with its somewhat intractable nature. Unlike the transverse flute, which allows its players many kinds of nuances and tonal colors, a recorder has basically only two aural states, sound and silence, on and off—something like the switches inside a computer chip and about equally supple and humane.

And yet, the recorder was counted among the instruments of seduction by the painters of the Italian Renaissance. Many a sixteenth-century painting of a bacchanal contains a symbolic recorder (along with other things meant to signify pleasure) somewhere within its frame. Frans Brüggen revived that seductiveness by indeed *playing* the instrument, rather than merely brandishing it like some Venetian cupid; and in so doing he managed to rouse his audiences to heights of enthusiasm rarely seen in the calm, contemplative circles of the musical antiquarians.

Long legs nonchalantly crossed, holding the recorder at an odd and slightly defiant angle to his mouth, Brüggen would treat the favorite Telemann sonatas of the amateur player crowd to the most astonishing kinds of metamorphoses. Abjuring the ticky-tocky style popular with Baroque performers in the recently elapsed fifties, Brüggen coaxed nuances and shadings from his instrument that few would have imagined possible heretofore. A hundred kinds of instrumental attacks, a thousand kinds of ways to shape a group of notes together, seemed to issue forth from the recorder's narrow bore. Nothing stood still or grew stolid: in the fast movements

Brüggen's incredible technique allowed sixteenth notes to cascade into the hall at breakneck speed. In slower passages, the sustained notes would rise disquietingly from the correct pitch, touch a point about a quarter-tone above the center, and sink back again. The little whistle heaved and sighed like a wood nymph in the embrace of some ardent faun.

The Brüggen *maniera* quickly revolutionized the teaching and playing of the recorder and its music, and not always for the better. Scores of young, aspiring virtuosi took to sticking the recorder at unusual angles to their faces and to playing every long note with a roller-coaster swell in the middle. Controversies flamed at weekend recorder workshops as to whether the celebrated hallmarks of the Brüggen playing style were truly founded in Baroque performance practice. Frans Brüggen himself defended many of his ways from the august podium of a visiting professorship at Harvard. There (and elsewhere) he was able to explain that many of the seemingly audacious things he did with a recorder were simply the application of precepts from seventeenth- and eighteenth-century performance treatises.

But like every good artist, Brüggen applied the basic precepts his own way. The spirit of contradiction coursed hot within his veins, and so he took every possible clue from the old manuals which would enable him to build a performing style that would be different from the Dolmetsch workshops, different from the Amsterdam conservatory, different from the polite, isn't-it-nice-weather-we're-having manner of the official chamber orchestras. Different!

Ironically, his originality spawned a host of Frans clones just a few years later. It is flattering for any performer to realize that he is the object of imitation and emulation. For someone with Brüggen's rebellious and individualistic temperament it must have been infuriating as well.

Controversies and camp-followers notwithstanding, the Brüggen legacy has permanently transformed and deepened our understanding of the recorder and its literature. It had been too easy, even for those who loved early music, to consign the recorder to the slag-heap of music history. The instrument's peculiar overtone structure and limited dynamic range made it seem more often than not just plain inadequate for the transmission of serious musical thought. By developing the inherent technical possibilities of the recorder to their maximum, and by applying a superior musical intelligence to every tiny detail of performance practice, Brüggen showed us that recorder playing could be as stimulating and rewarding an activity as anything else, and not just for the performer. And he proved that there is really no such thing as an "inferior" instrument; there are only players without enough imagination.

Brüggen's keen sense of opposition and contradiction led him to many of his important discoveries in the field of recorder technique. Those same character traits also led him to question many other *idées reçues* of the musical order. He became interested in avant-garde contemporary music, and cultivated friendships with some eminent contemporary composers; one day during his Baroque seminar at Harvard he taunted his students by playing the solo piece that avant-garde composer Luciano Berio had written for him, and defying his listeners to pick out the mistakes he was deliberately inserting in Berio's hard-to-read score. His involvement with the Dutch counter-culture movement led to some unusual moments during his recitals: at a concert with the trio Sour Cream (Brüggen plus two of his student-colleagues, Kees Boeke and Walter van Hauwe), the last piece featured a Keystone-Kops chase around the concert stage.

A season or two later, the same trio performed in Boston more determined than ever to *épater les bourgeois*. While Kees and Walter played Telemann duos, Brüggen wandered onto the Jordan Hall stage, donned a pair of dark sunglasses, stretched himself out on a chaise longue, and nonchalantly began reading a copy of the daily newspaper. The event provoked an indignant editorial from the *Boston Globe* a couple of days later. At least some members of the educated classes, who often brush their teeth in the morning to the strains of canned Vivaldi, had failed to get the satirical point. *Les bourgeois* — or some of them, at any rate — were not amused.

Brüggen himself seemed less and less amused by the idea of giving solo recitals on the recorder. He still commands astronomical fees for those appearances, but nowadays his heart and soul are elsewhere. Some of his colleagues view Brüggen's recent activity as a conductor with a measure of mistrust. The recorder virtuoso's decision to found (and even in part to autofinance) his own orchestra was greeted in some quarters with the skeptical jeers accorded Secretary of State William Seward as he arranged to purchase Alaska from the Russians.

As it turned out, both the Alaska purchase and the Orchestra of the Eighteenth Century (as Brüggen has named it) were worthwhile undertakings, despite the forbidding scale of each. The new orchestra, as its name suggests, is intended for the performance of pre-classical and classical period music. Like many Baroque specialists, Brüggen has become increasingly drawn to the style period just following the one he originally specialized in. The orchestra plays Rameau, Mozart, and even early Beethoven, applying to those later masters the same kinds of approaches that worked so well with Lully and Vivaldi and Bach. The instrumentalists have been recruited from the first ranks of the younger Baroque players; their instruments replicate those in use at the end of the eighteenth century; and the playing style is derived in large part from our historical knowledge about orchestras of that period. More important (and here is the main difference between this orchestra and others that have delved into the Mozart-Haydn repertoire with period instruments), the performances are strongly personal statements about the music rather than efficient sight-readings. It is now possible, given the increasing professionalism of early music players, to rehearse Mozart's *Jupiter* Symphony in the morning and produce a technically adequate disk recording in the afternoon. That surface approach cannot, however, do justice to the "inside" of a genuine musical masterpiece like the *Jupiter*. Too many important things must be left undiscussed and undecided.

Brüggen's current performances reflect a lot of hard work on a myriad of small details: tone color, balances, the articulation of individual notes in inner voices. The result, though, is anything but dry and pedagogical. Familiar works (like the late Mozart symphonies) seem to come alive again, revealing themselves as though for the first time. Hearing that music with this ensemble is something like seeing a familiar Old Master painting on its return from a thorough cleaning and restoration. Colors that had been dimmed and dulled by layers of grit and varnish can now reappear with their true intensity and expressive impact. We are now hearing many "early music" performances of Mozart and Haydn (Beethoven and Schubert as well), offered by people who apprenticed first in Baroque music. Frans Brüggen's experiments in this direction must be counted among the most satisfying of the lot.

Brüggen's success with Mozart depends on those same personal qualities that were evident in his recorder playing: the refusal to take anything for granted, the willingness to take risks, and the untiring search for solutions that probe beyond convention and lazy self-evidence.*

We have noted earlier that the decision to make one's life in early music has as much to do with the present as it does with the past. Nowhere is that more evident than in Frans Brüggen's career. Restless, dissatisfied, probingly intelligent, he has consistently refused to play by the established rules. His search for other precepts and other principles came from an inner need to do things his own way. The music of the distant past has been a means toward a personal end. Frans Brüggen the surgeon would have invented an outlandish but brilliantly successful technique to transplant some obscure but necessary vital organ. Frans Brüggen the auto mechanic would probably have set about redesigning the internal combustion engine, just to show the world how badly it had been done in the first place. It was a loss to the hospitals and the garages of this planet, but we music lovers can be glad: young Frans picked up neither a scalpel nor a monkey wrench as his tool for getting even with the world's dullards, but a Baroque recorder!

* Nikolaus Harnoncourt's recent series of Mozart projects is equally probing and unconventional; but Harnoncourt has been working mainly with modern orchestras in his Mozart enterprise, while Brüggen has recruited an ensemble of period instruments.

XI

Gustav Leonhardt

*N*EVER was there such a difference between the outer appearance and the inner self! The way this man inhabits his body recalls the epigram about a famous French writer: *"Victor Hugo, c'est un homme qui se prend pour Victor Hugo."* In this case, you might say that Gustav Leonhardt (b. 1928) is a man who resembles a memorial statue of Gustav Leonhardt.*

It may seem unfair and trivial to begin discussing one of the greatest performing artists of the twentieth century with a flippant remark about the way he looks. I do so because I am convinced that the quantities of idiotic things that have been said in print about Leonhardt have more to do with how he appears than with how he plays. During the Rameau anniversary year of 1983, Leonhardt appeared in France as a conductor, leading Sigiswald Kuijken's La Petite Bande in several all-Rameau concerts. The performance I heard that summer in Toulouse was a wholly extraordinary experience: Leonhardt shaped Rameau's phrases, breathed life into the dance movements, underlined the unusual harmonic turns, clarified the orchestral textures—did everything necessary to make Rameau's thorny, hermetic music sound vibrant and alive.

* See the Photograph Section for a picture of Leonhardt.

[67]

Did the professional music critics notice? I saw only one review, one that took Leonhardt to task for his "mechanical, staccato" style of conducting! It was as though the writer had simply not heard the music — instead, he apparently substituted his visual impressions for aural ones.

Dismiss the French critic if you will (poor France is not noted for the acuity and competence of its music writers), but you will have a harder time ignoring the summary evaluation of Leonhardt as performer in the 1980 *New Grove's Dictionary of Music and Musicians:*

> *Despite much subtle rhythmic nuance and tasteful ornamentation, Leonhardt's playing tends to be rather sober and at times even severe.*

Now there's an authoritative source! College freshmen will be looking up the Leonhardt article for years to come, and they will dutifully report in their term papers that Leonhardt's playing tends, alas, to be somewhat sober and severe.

The problem is, Leonhardt's musicianship is woefully, shamefully misserved by these kinds of statements. For if it is true that cogitation and reflection have played a large part in the shaping of Leonhardt's interpretive approach, it is also just as true that the emotions are an intensely important component of his performances. Rarely has one heard such deeply felt Bach, such passionate Frescobaldi. To hear Leonhardt's recording of Johann Jakob Froberger's "Meditation sur ma mort future" ("Meditation on my future death") is to contemplate man's deepest questions about his own destiny; and to witness Leonhardt's way with Rameau's theater music is, contrariwise, to relive the world of Baroque movement and dance in one's very bones. The range of feeling, the scope of passion that Leonhardt is able to evoke, both as harpsichordist and as conductor, are every bit as impressive as his finely honed analytic skills, his profound understanding of music history, and his superb ear.

To understand how Leonhardt's approach to Baroque music has revolutionized the attitudes of an entire performing generation, one has to reflect on what harpsichord playing tended to be like in the decade or so before the Dutch master's arrival on the scene. The first twentiety-century wave of interest in early music had spawned its own style of Baroque playing—and that style was based essentially on two things: first, a reaction against the excessive self-indulgence of Romantic soloism; and second, a taste for cool, abstract, "objective" performances.

As we have already noted, the early music movement began to take hold at the same time and for many of the same reasons as much avant-garde contemporary art. Both the avant-gardists and the early music devotees of the twenties and thirties, for example, were reacting against the immediate past and its values: the battle cry of *Neue Sachlichkeit* (new objectivity) was heard on both the creative and interpretive fronts.

Thus it was that "enlightened" performance of composers like Bach was supposed to hew as closely to the printed page as possible. Playing the notes in strict mechanical sequence was definitely "in," and considered to be the authentic way of approaching the music of the eighteenth century. Expressive devices like rubato, arpeggiation, ornament, and dynamic variation were generally ruled "out," and consigned to the scrap-heap of late-nineteenth-century excess. By the late 1950s, the pioneer performances of Wanda Landowska, whose roots lay so obviously in the world of nineteenth-century pianism, were considered to be irrevocably antiquated and *vieux jeu*.

Then along came Leonhardt (and Harnoncourt, and some illustrious others). The new generation of Baroque specialists examined the primary source materials anew, without the anti-Romantic biases of the previous generation. Lo and behold! It became obvious on reading performance treatises, theoretical studies, and musical criticism from the eighteenth century—and also from careful contemplation of the musical scores—that Bach was not the operator of some cosmic sewing machine, but the author of some of the most expressive and emotion-laden music known to man. This in itself was not a new insight; after all, Mendelssohn and Schumann (and Landowska herself) had known as much. But it was reintroduced into the music world's consciousness at an appropriate moment, and was accompanied by some fresh, thorough investigations of old performance techniques as described in the seventeenth- and eighteenth-century treatises.

What Leonhardt did for the harpsichord was, above all, to reintroduce an expressive vocabulary for the instrument, a way or ways of making it sing and breathe, sigh and dance. The harpsichord can be a frustrating tool; expressive devices that are second nature to any singer or string player (or pianist) are impossible to achieve on its keyboard. The harpsichord has a one-way attack: the sound of a note is loudest at the beginning, and the decay is quick. No expressive swells or swoops are available to the keyboard player of any persuasion, and the harpsichordist must in addition come to terms with the inability of the instrument to vary significantly the loudness or softness of a string.

Leonhardt's solution (not simply his, since it was well grounded in historical keyboard practice) was to cultivate a playing style of extraordinary rhythmic suppleness and variety. What the harpsichord could not furnish in varied intensity of sound would be compensated for by a maximum of nuance in phrasing. The placement of each note in time, as each note related both to the underlying rhythmic structure of the work and to the other, neighboring notes nearby, became the crucial element in the transmission of musical intent and expression.

If you are a violinist (for example), you may choose to play the last pulse of a rhythmic cycle (the upbeat) significantly softer than the strong beat that follows (the downbeat); you may use an up bow on weaker beats, and a down bow on stronger ones. Such tactics are of no avail on the harpsichord — neither loud-soft nor push-pull are legal moves in the early keyboard player's game.

The automatic-pilot style once in favor a generation ago counseled the harpsichordist to ignore the demands of rhythmic articulation and to plow ahead in the strictest measured time possible. This was held to be an elegant way of purifying the music.

Leonhardt's solution (once again, he did not invent it — he simply paid close attention to the writings of musicians like Couperin) was to create a *space* between the upbeat and the downbeat, a microscopically small but expressively crucial bit of silence that allowed the mind and the ear to register the different meanings of "last beat" and "first beat" in the musical discourse.

Similarly, Leonhardt applied the techniques of space and silence, of accelerando and rallentando, to the melodic line as a whole; an instrument that is incapable of sustaining a sound was heard to "sing" its lines as never before. And not just one line: Leonhardt's grasp of the contrapuntal and harmonic dimensions of Baroque styles made for performances of unusual clarity, in which every inner voice seemed to have its own special life, its own unique being. When Leonhardt is playing or conducting at the top of his form, you get the impression that you are hearing the music composed in front of you. Like the other great artists in this field (or in any other), he is able to release the hidden energy latent in the printed musical page, and to direct it toward the souls of his hearers.

Why, then, this persistent misapprehension of Gustav Leonhardt? Why the often repeated cavils about his supposed dryness and severity? His Dutch-gothic face and reserved personal manner certainly have something to do with it. Another reason, I think, has to do with the general public's (current) unreadiness to deal with soloists who try above all else to express the music rather than some notion or image of themselves as virtuosi.

In the world of standard repertoire, where we all hear the same handful of pieces a hundred times over, it becomes important for an aspiring virtuoso soloist or conductor to establish a personal mark on the well-known works he or she is called on to perform. Sometimes that personal stamp comes from genuine conviction and musical insight; sometimes it is a more or less counterfeit simulation of passion and engagement. But in any case, the aspiring soloist in the world of concert-music-at-large has to market his or her persona, and in ways not too dissimilar from those used to create movie stars or American political "leaders."

Here, on the other hand, is the kind of man who simply refuses to "sell" himself, or even to hire some vice president in charge of marketing the Leonhardt persona and product. He will never appear on the cover of *People* magazine, and he couldn't care less. I do not think that this sublime disdain for the mechanics of the profit-seeking marketplace comes from any special anti-Establishment point of view (after all, he recently confided with evident relish how much he enjoys talking to the Queen of the Netherlands in the antiquated grammatical forms still employed at the court). His aloofness is really that of the pre-modern, aristocratic gentleman for whom any contact with the world of trade and finance is vaguely degrading and distasteful.

He refuses to promote himself. But what a marvelous, what an eloquent advocate he is of the *music* he performs. It is the voice of the composer that Leonhardt so conscientiously searches out; it is the inherent expressive power of the work before him that he seeks to communicate. Are his performances "authentic"? Are they exact recreations of the playing styles in vogue two to three hundred years ago? I don't know. What is important to me (and, I suppose, to other listeners as well) is the passionately honest, probing quality of everything Leonhardt does. In a world of glitter, tinsel, and opportunistic mediocrity, Gustav Leonhardt is a Diogenes holding up the lantern of musical truth.

XII

Singers, or the Main Difficulty*

I hope, therefore, that Mr. Dolmetsch will dig up plenty of genuine medieval music for us. . . . The quality of the performances, which has always been surprisingly good, considering the strangeness of the instruments, continues to improve. The vocal music is still the main difficulty. The singers, with their heads full of modern "effects", shew but a feeble sense of the accuracy of intonation and tenderness of expression required by the pure vocal harmonies of the old school. Without a piano to knock their songs into them they seem at a loss; and the only vocalist whom I felt inclined to congratulate was the counter-tenor, the peculiarity of whose voice had saved him from the lot of the drawing-room songster.

—GEORGE BERNARD SHAW**

*T*HERE is no way to tell if George Bernard Shaw was right about most of his musical judgments; after all, he wrote before the

* Many of the singers discussed in this chapter are pictured in the Photograph Section.
** February 7, 1897; quoted in *The Great Composers: Reviews and Bombardments by Bernard Shaw* (Berkeley, 1978), p. 320.

age of recorded sound, and the performances he discussed are remembered now only because of what he said about them.

Concerning singers of early music, though, he was probably dead
accurate. What is amazing (and amusing) about this passage, first
published in 1897, is first of all its precocious insight into the special
nature of early music interpretation; and second, how very contemporary his complaints about the habitual mismatch between singers
and early instruments do sound. *Plus ça change* . . .

For if in recent years we have begun to hear a generation of young
singers both enthusiastic about, and well trained in, the pre-Romantic repertoire, the changes in approach to vocal style have been slow
in coming—much slower than those in the instrumental field. A
craftsman can measure the dimensions of an old recorder or violin,
carefully reproducing in his or her own, modern instrument the
characteristics of the antique model. A present-day recorder player
or violinist can replicate with a rather high degree of fidelity many
performance techniques of two centuries ago: the player has those
good instruments (copies or antiques) to practice on, and some detailed "how-to" manuals from the period available for study.

How different is the singer's lot! Unlike the aspiring harpsichordist, who can study and play on old keyboards, the young soprano has
no external model for comparison, no moldering Baroque diva
whose bones she can profitably exhume. Her instrument is in her
body, her instrument *is* her body, and the early vocal treatises she has
pored over in search of guidance (if she has a scholarly streak) can tell
her so little without some living sound from the past as a guide. Oh,
for just one scratchy 78-rpm disk from the sixteenth century of
Giulio Caccini's singing! For just one battered cylinder recording of
the twelfth-century troubadour Marcabru declaiming his poems!
Those sounds have gone forever, and no amount of writing from the
past, no matter how lucid, can ever replace their vanished eloquence.

Small wonder, then, that many early music performances, even
nowadays, manifest a certain schizoid quality when both voices and
instruments are present. On the one hand, the instrumentalists favor
a lighter, cooler sound; many small articulations within a longer
phrase; and a near-total absence of vibrato. On the other hand, the

singers rely on maximum volume, long unbroken lines, and a thick, creamy wobble on every possible note in order to achieve their effect. Worse (in the worst cases, that is), the instrumentalists seem to be playing for God (or for each other), while the vocal soloists stretch and strain their public selves like contestants at the Miss America pageant, or the participants in a gala night at some remote provincial opera house.

The gap is closing rapidly, and those kinds of performance are already becoming much more unusual, thanks to the newer generation of singers. Yet the rate of change to a more transparent and appropriate style has been slow, and the pioneers in the world of vocal style and early singing techniques have had to be even more courageous, even more daring than their instrumentalist colleagues. For no other instrument arouses such violent passions as the voice, and in no other area of musical activity is there such a mix of personal risk and reactionary defensiveness, of love and paranoia.

The techniques required for florid passage work in early music are not generally taught to modern-day singers. Indeed, the current trend toward all-resonators-open, all-stops-out singing in large halls makes light, clean passage work a very hard thing to do well or "authentically." The voice teachers of the seventeenth century counseled their students to produce florid ornaments in the throat.* That technique is anathema to most conservatory teachers of our day. So the singer who wants to cut through the jungle of received ideas about singing in order to experience early music afresh has had to risk exile, scorn, and isolation from vocalist colleagues.

---

* For instance: "I say that the voice is only a sound caused by the minute and controlled expression of air in the throat. . . . The place where diminutions are made . . . is the same place where the voice is formed, that is, the cartilage called the *cimbalara* . . . which, when it is constricted or dilated by the sinews . . . breaks and strikes the air so minutely that the desired singing is produced by everyone" (Giovanni Camillo Maffei, "Letter on Singing," 1552; translated and edited by Carol MacClintock in *Readings in the History of Music in Performance,* Bloomington, 1979). A performer who is willing to take these kinds of instructions seriously is well on his or her way toward becoming an early music person!

ALFRED DELLER

Had Alfred Deller (1912–1979) been a tenor or a baritone, he might never have been able to make his mark in the concert world of the 1940s and 1950s. But since the countertenor, or male alto, voice had next to no role in music composed after 1800, it was perhaps no accident that Deller was able to achieve so much during a period when few other kinds of "early music" singing were attempted by performers or accepted by the general public. The "lot of the drawing-room songster" was happily not Deller's, and the totally "other" quality of his voice kept him from clashing head on with the singing establishment. His youthful grounding in English cathedral choir lore (those choruses have never stopped singing their Renaissance repertoire, nor have they ever abandoned the use of male altos) certainly helped him find his way in the music of the distant past. But the church choir world is one thing, and for all that is wonderful about the English tradition, Deller seems to have come into his main interpretive strengths very much on his own.

Certainly there was no precedent for his magnificent achievement in the heretofore timid world of English musical antiquarianism (nor has anyone done quite the same things since in the English-language solo repertoire). His was a falsetto singing voice; naturally a baritone, he cultivated the high register above the break, unlike some modern male altos who have tried to achieve a fully supported sound in the range above tenor. With the very "artificial" instrument at his disposal, Deller was able to make sounds of extraordinary beauty and delicacy; even in his later years, when his voice had darkened and deepened, he could astonish hearers with the range of vocal colors at his command.

Deller was an instinctive man, and every inch a singer — so much so that his second career as director and conductor never equaled in musical glory what he was able to achieve as a soloist. Then, too, Deller was miles ahead of many of his collaborators — the other singers in his consort came from the world of "normal" music, and it showed.

Yet nothing, but nothing, could stop Deller from storming the heavens on a good singing day. His intense and intimate relation to English poetry gave him the means to sing with the most profound and deeply felt emotion. Since he had reflected long and hard on the strengths and limitations of his unusual voice, he was able to turn every last vocal possibility (and even a number of his weaknesses) into tools for sculpting a musical line. Every nuance, every shade of feeling in a poem found its corresponding coloration in Deller's sung delivery.

Deller's feeling for poetry, his ability to meld words and music into an expressive whole, made him something of a Renaissance man. And his precious gift for making a poem live through song could well serve as a model for the current generation, despite the real progress that has been made these last few years in early music vocal style.

Detractors called his style "mannered"; and the younger generation of English singers has tended toward a much more neutral, emotionally cool manner of text declamation. The current trend toward a more reserved performing style has certainly helped to clarify polyphonic music and to show that older repertoire can be effective without demagogic screaming.

But progress is not simply linear, and if the young school of English singers has gained much in the battle for a purified early music vocal style, it has lost something as well.

Standards of vocal performance are overall much higher now than in Deller's day. But the careful, cleanly wrought performances we often hear from specialized ensembles in this decade can on occasion be faulted: they fail, at times, to evoke the intrinsic emotion or affect implied by the sung texts. We need to learn how to serve the poetry more, as Deller did, and to make

> *. . . the lines*
> *That young men, tossing on their beds,*
> *Rhymed out in love's despair*
> *To flatter beauty's ignorant ear*

come alive again in our performances!

CHANGING STYLES

During the first two-thirds of the twentieth century, only a handful of concert singers devoted themselves exclusively (or at any rate for the most part) to the interpretation of pre-Romantic music. Aside from Deller, whose countertenor voice more or less precluded his involvement with other repertoires, audiences learned about Medieval, Renaissance, and Baroque vocal music from singers whose training and principal activities had been in other styles.

Some of those singers were nonetheless intelligent, capable artists who gravitated to the music of the distant past because their voices, or temperaments, or a combination of the two, seemed suited to these kinds of works.

Although the parameters of early music singing style have been changing rapidly in the last few years, the archival recorded performances by the best of these pioneers can still bring us much pleasure and delight. No one, for instance, has sung the troubadours' songs with quite the same magical love for Provençal poetry as Chanterelle del Vasto, on an old recording for an obscure French label, Boîte à Musique. No one has bettered the now-defunct Luca Marenzio ensemble in certain things essential to the Italian madrigal repertoire: rhetorical flair and Latinate dramatic gesture. And what discophile can forget the voices of Paul Derenne and Hugues Cuénod singing "Zefiro torna" on those ancient shellac recordings of Monteverdi's music by Nadia Boulanger?

Those voices and those performances were among the oases of intelligence and insight in a concert world dominated by other kinds of values. There were, of course, other such moments of grace, but not perhaps all that many. For every Hugues Cuénod, whose exemplary phrasing and sense of proportion helped us to discover the world of Renaissance and Baroque solo song, there was a platoon of recital tenors ready to massacre a couple of "Arie antiche" at the start of a concert, before proceeding to the real business at hand: singing Verdi and Puccini as loudly as possible. For every Theresa Stich-Randall there were battalions of imperial sopranos anxious to turn Bach and Handel into offensive weapons against the clients in the last row.

The most radical attempt to turn that situation around came in the mid-1960s, from the soloists of the Studio der Fruehen Musik (whose ensemble work is discussed in Chapter VI), and most especially from the group's female singer, Andrea von Ramm. Von Ramm, like Deller, has a voice that simply will not fit into most "normal" concert-hall situations. Her natural instrument is very low, and she produces her high notes as though she were a man singing falsetto. Her unusual technique puts over three usable octaves at her disposal; it also contributes to her very personal, spooky, and androgynous vocal color.

Or perhaps the expression "vocal colors" would be more suitable. For von Ramm cultivated not one kind of singing style, but many (including cabaret song). The performances of Studio ranged over several centuries' worth of music, and Andrea tried to find a way of using the voice appropriate to each style.

Sometimes her voice would be dark and covered; sometimes bright and forward. Sometimes one would hear mainly high or middle or low resonances; sometimes a blend of registers and resonators. Sometimes the emission would be clear and vibratoless; at other moments there would be a fast or a slow vibrato, a little or a lot. It may seem self-evident that the voice is to be used differently, depending on whether one is singing Machaut or Palestrina or Lully, but Andrea was among the first to take the challenge of style differentiation very seriously. Her lively, charismatic stage presence and her understanding of the way language colors the singing voice (she is also a professor of rhetoric and declamation at the University of Basel) helped win over concert audiences as Studio hopped from trouvère melodies to English lute songs in the course of a single recital. In later seasons, as the group specialized more and more in Medieval monody, von Ramm's way with varied coloring and shading of the voice helped sustain Studio's increasingly ambitious and demanding style experiments.

Studio was influenced by many a practice common to traditional singers in the Mediterranean basin; and it was not the only group to experiment with unusual ways of singing in the Medieval and Renaissance repertoire. In England there was a brief vogue for singing Dufay in the style of Balkan folk music. "I think the whole concept of vibratoless singing began with John Beckett and Michael Morrow," reminisces bass-baritone David Thomas. "I remember when they first began putting together Musica Reservata. They got a bunch of us singers together and played us these records of Bulgarian peasants wailing through their noses.

" 'We want it like this,' they said. No vibrato, harsh nasal sound, strict tempo, no expressive nuance. We performed all sorts of Medieval and Renaissance repertoire in that way; of course, some pieces worked better than others."

Perhaps Musica Reservata's experiments in vocal style have worn less well than other things from the same period. Still, its featured soloist Jantina Noorman's way with every vocal color under the sun taught us a great deal about the potential of the human voice — and today, the idea that "classical" singers can learn important techniques from the world of folklore and non-European art music is no longer such a heresy. In other contexts, both Montserrat Figueras and her sister, Pilar, have evolved a way of singing Medieval and Renaissance music from Spain and neighboring countries that owes much to the living traditions of Spanish folklore.

And in another kind of repertoire, the virtuoso English tenor Nigel Rogers owes some of his extraordinary suppleness and brilliance in Baroque *passaggi* to his study of Indian vocal music and voice production. Rogers's best-known work is in Baroque music, but he has been active in still earlier repertoires as well; he was associated in its earlier days with the Studio der Fruehen Musik.

Even nowadays, however, the tenor-in-the-street is unlikely to see any connection at all between Monteverdi and South Indian ragas. Yet the florid passage work essential for early music, described earlier, is still an important part of voice production in many other kinds of music — think of your favorite flamenco singer, or of Greek or Arabic popular song.

Since our concert work is so sealed up, so insulated from those kinds of musical influences, we have become alienated as well from our own past, and from the ways in which our own musical civilization resembled those of others. The door to cross-cultural exchange and insight has been opened just a crack in the areas of Medieval and Renaissance music. But the Baroque repertoire, which is closer to our time, less exotic and "other," and full of still-familiar masterworks — that repertoire has been slower to undergo change and renewal of its vocal practices. Even as the sounds of Baroque violins and oboes have begun infiltrating the musical public's consciousness, the resistance to similar rethinkings of vocal sound has been strong. The "early instrument" version of some standard oratorio, featuring instrumental techniques from 1750, and vocal techniques from 1950, is still very much with us, and will probably remain so for at least another decade, while the singers catch up with the players.

Some fine singers of Baroque music have nonetheless graced the early instrument world with their collaboration. Nigel Rogers, now increasingly active as a conductor, is a master of early seventeenth-century French and (especially) Italian monodic singing. He manages to combine an extraordinarily supple and fluid sound with the dramatic vigor and presence necessary to make those repertoires come alive. The Dutch baritone Max von Egmond is a frequent collaborator in performances directed by Harnoncourt and Leonhardt, and his exquisite sense of musical nuance is matched only by his consummate professionalism. I once saw von Egmond turn in a magical performance as Aeneas in Henry Purcell's *Dido and Aeneas* with just one walk-through of the staging before curtain time. His most enduring contributions, though, are his thoughtful, sensitive readings of Baroque solo repertoire. Von Egmond manages to make his small-to-medium-sized voice express an infinite variety of expressive shadings. In ways that recall the earlier career of tenor Hugues Cuénod, he achieves the finest possible results through intelligence, hard work, and unusual flair.

In anyone's hierarchy of outstanding Baroque singers, the German tenor Kurt Equiluz must occupy an elevated rank. Although his career has ranged farther afield than the seventeenth and eighteenth centuries, Equiluz has a special gift for Bach's vocal music. His interpretations of the Evangelist roles in the major Bach oratorios have renewed our understanding of German-language recitative. The supple, speaking quality that characterizes Equiluz's work in the Bach passions recalls the variations of nuance and articulation obtainable by a good Baroque violinist using a period instrument and bow. More important still, his singing of Bach is intimately linked to the speech rhythms, to the ebb and flow, of the German language itself. The stentorian, public-monument style of oratorio singing that was the official way for so long in this century is replaceable — and has been replaced — by something better.

ENGLISH SINGERS: A NEW REGIONAL STYLE

"The idea of regional performance style is so important for old music," says Andrea von Ramm. "You have to differentiate between German and Italian, between Italian and French, and so on. Even the dialects of the same language have a tremendous impact on the sound of a performance. There wasn't just one way to perform Old French, there were a hundred! And each one had its own, different kind of word music.

"What is less widely recognized," she continues, "is that nowadays we, too, have our regional styles. Our contemporary performances of early music are strongly influenced by our countries of origin. Look at the current crop of English singers, for instance: they share a common approach to performance, and they all seem to have such wonderful control, such beautiful singing tones." *

One of the most striking developments in the early music field has indeed been the appearance on the scene of so many fine, well-trained English singers. Some of the new generation have managed to achieve near-superstar status after only a few years of professional activity, thus giving the lie to dire predictions by old-line critics that light, cool singing voices could never find a large public in the concert world. The soprano Emma Kirkby, for example, whose pure, clear voice and careful diction have come to epitomize the new English school, can now boast of larger record sales than Joan Sutherland.

Even more important than the presence of bright solo personali-

* Interview with the author, September 1983.

ties like Emma Kirkby's is the existence of a pool of capable, well-trained people in all voice categories. Much of the early music repertoire (from the Renaissance especially but earlier and later as well) is vocal chamber music, and until very recently we have simply not had the performing means to hear vocal chamber music done well. Imagine, if you will, a land in which every violinist trained only to play solo concerti. In such an unfortunate place, it would be impossible to obtain a good performance of string quartets by Haydn or Beethoven or anyone else. Since every fiddle player would rehearse the Paganini and Tchaikowsky concerti from infancy, every attempt to form a string quartet would be doomed to failure. Each first violinist would manage to make every work in the repertoire sound like an inadequate, poorly conceived violin concerto.

Not dissimilar was the sorry fate of Renaissance part music until just a few years ago. A gifted soloist here and there does not a madrigal consort make, and the attempts to perform Renaissance polyphony one-on-a-part, which were made with soloists from the oratorio and recital world, often failed entirely.

The English "regional style" of early music singing has changed all that. It is now possible for us to hear English and Italian madrigals, French chansons, and similar works from the fifteenth to seventeenth centuries in a much more appropriate guise. No longer are we condemned to hear five or six frustrated soloists each straining to outdo the other, each attempting to impress and excel with some unusual personal color or quirk of temperament, each putting himself or herself forward at the expense of the whole. It is now possible to hear in early part music the interplay of voices, the interweaving of musical lines and textures, which is the essence of enjoyment and comprehension in these styles.

(Even the world of Baroque oratorio is beginning to change. You can now hear performances of Handel in which the soloists match each other, and the music, much better than they did just a few years ago.)

The regional performance style of the young Englishmen and women has in a few short years broadened and deepened our understanding of early vocal music (the phenomenally high level of sight-

reading skills in England plays its role, too; we get many new recordings from English singers in part because they are able to churn them
out so fast).

It is perhaps no coincidence that so many of our best early music
singers are English. That country has always managed to ally respect
for the past with quirky individualism in many lines of endeavor, and
those are two very important attributes of early music people. More
important still, the English have maintained their enthusiasm for
choral singing and for vocal part music for many centuries. There was
an alternative to opera singing available in England at any moment
over the last several hundred years, another way of imagining and
employing the human voice. So many good singers, trained in so
many fine cathedral choirs, familiar in each generation with some of
the Renaissance masterpieces, were bound to bear fruit in the present
concert-hall revival of early music.

The current abundance of good English performers and performances has come with a price tag, nonetheless: many listeners have
remarked on the trend toward a neutral, homogenized kind of performance ethos evident in the work of some English groups. When
such wildly different composers as Machaut and Monteverdi begin
to sound alike, we may reasonably impute the likeness to something
in the performances — to the English regional style of this moment
— rather than to the original musical texts. All the fluency, all the
tasteful restraint that made those ensemble performances possible
has exacted a toll in the undue sameness that has been known to
overtake some English performances of early music.

Still, the English singers have given us many wonderful moments of
pleasure; and they have taught us many invaluable things. Thanks to
their efforts, and to the work of singing colleagues in other countries,
we are managing to overcome the "main difficulty" described by
GBS. We can now hear early music performances in which the
singers' voices match the instruments, and each other; in which good
tuning is a normal state of affairs rather than a miraculous happen-
stance; in which "tenderness of expression" has replaced the philoso-
phy of frontal assault. For all these musical gifts we can be grateful.
"The quality of the performances . . . continues to improve."

XIII

Amateurs

*T*HE music and musical instruments of the distant past have
lured many an impressionable adolescent into an oddball professional career. And this book focuses in the main on those musicians
who have dedicated their whole working lives to making early music
live again. Yet the professionals represent only the tip of an iceberg.
The submerged majority of the early music movement consists of a
mass of amateur players and singers, ranging in skill from near-total
ineptitude to the most dazzling accomplishment. The many thousands of nonprofessional harpsichordists, madrigal singers, gambists,
krumhorn players, and so forth who make up this not-so-silent majority are every bit as important to the vitality of the early music
movement as the handful of professionals who earn their daily bread
by resurrecting the past. And in some concrete, definable ways, the
amateurs, by their enthusiasm and their force of numbers, have left a
permanent mark on our contemporary musical existence. Take, for
instance, the miraculous, modern-day resurrection of an instrument
that music history tried to forget: the recorder.

As remarked earlier in our discussion of Frans Brüggen, the recorder is quite an intractable instrument. Like an organ pipe, it is just
a tuned whistle. Musical Europe gave up trying to deal with this

venerable but inflexible tool about halfway through the eighteenth century; art music thereafter had a place only for the more amenable *flauto traverso*.

The recorder's resurrection began a century and a half later, as the early music revival movement was just getting under way. In 1905, Arnold Dolmetsch bought an eighteenth-century recorder for two pounds at a Sotheby's auction. Fourteen years later, in 1919, he lost his favorite recorder, an antique Bressan, at a London train station; the mishap spurred him to start making modern copies. The twentieth-century recorder revival was launched. A powerful wing of the early music movement, based on amateur recorder playing in groups, was to grow up in just a few years following the appearance of the Dolmetsch copies.

The recorder had an immediate appeal to amateur musicians for several reasons. To begin with, it is easy (deceptively easy) to generate a sound on this instrument. You just infuse some air into its mouthpiece, and a noise comes out. The transverse flute, on the other hand, needs to be coaxed into making a sound; the player has to create a vibrating air column with his lips, and that kind of skill can take a long time to acquire. The recorder's fingering system is simpler than that found on any modern wind instrument. And all the members of the recorder family, from the smallest and highest pitched to the largest and deepest, are fingered exactly the same way. It is thus relatively easy to set up recorder ensembles among players with limited skills and training.

And so the recorder has become a pedagogical tool in hundreds of school systems from Dubuque to Delft. Many a youngster has received the first taste of do-it-yourself instrumental performance by tootling "Au clair de la lune" or "Yankee Doodle" together with the other kids in the recorder class. These exercises are supposed to prepare our young for the headier pleasures of Beethoven or Michael Jackson, and sometimes they do.

The recorder has whistled its siren call into the ears of many adult amateurs: the hundreds of recorder clubs and recorder societies that can be found all over the Western world are a kind of musical subculture all to themselves. They allow ordinary citizens—

teachers, lawyers, housewives, musicologists, and the like — many of the pleasures obtainable through ensemble playing without the years of arduous preparation necessary to professionals. The Sunday afternoon sessions of Renaissance *danseries à 40* have certainly generated too many high overtones for comfort; the wildly out-of-tune recorder orchestra tweedling its way through a Palestrina motet can bring little pleasure to any third parties. But recorder clubs have brought satisfaction and personal contentment to many people since Dolmetsch first started manufacturing those early copies. And those circles of amateur music making continue to be places where people can discover the special joys and delights obtainable from the music of the distant past.

If the members of recorder societies, glee clubs, and similar organizations have turned so often and with such enthusiasm to the early music repertoire, it is with good reason. The amateur repertoire of the nineteenth and twentieth centuries has for the most part very little to do with the works we now enjoy in the concert hall. True, Schubert and Schumann and Bartók wrote fine things for amateurs; but in general, the music that is now written and conceived for nonprofessional performers is far inferior in content and craftsmanship to the finest products of our best composers. Look at what the average church choir sings on Sunday morning, or what children are expected to sing in public school music class, if you want some ready examples of our modern decadence.

It was not always so. The first commercial concert, offered to a fee-paying public, took place in England, in 1672. If you wanted musical entertainment prior to the Baroque era, and you weren't some nobleman with a private band, you generally had to manufacture the sounds yourself, or with a little help from your friends. Nothing pejorative attached to the Italian *dilettante* (someone who delights in the arts) when the word was new!

So it was that the part-time performers during the Renaissance (or to a lesser degree the Baroque era) had all kinds of wonderful music composed just for them by highly skilled and inventive authors. Almost the entire madrigal repertoire, for example, was written for amateurs — only a few virtuoso pieces from the late sixteenth and early seventeenth centuries were conceived for professional court singers. The finest and subtlest musical thoughts of Lassus and Monteverdi, of Marenzio and John Wilbye, were intended for and entrusted to the performing skills of amateur musicians. One can argue, with considerable justification, that today's amateur has even more compelling reasons to turn back in time than the professional. The fine music available to professionals covers the whole span of music history. But the amateurs must turn to the past to find lots of music that is both technically simple and spiritually vigorous. The Romantics and the moderns have not given them enough good compositions to play!

Indeed, if the "serious" composers of our own day wrote quantities of very appealing, highly significant works for part-time performers, there might be a lot more contemporary classical music in the air. But such is not the case. And as a result, many instrument makers of today are kept busy turning out modern reproductions of ancient musical tools for amateur players. The harpsichord makers would all be stockpiling their expensive wares were it not for the many part-time keyboard players — corporation executives, neurosurgeons, and others — willing and able to buy them. And all over Japan, twenty-four-hour automated factories continue to eject an endless stream of inexpensive, surprisingly well-made plastic recorders into the music classrooms of our planet.

The early music movement has not reached tidal-wave proportions, and it never will. But the presence of all these highly motivated amateur performers has a salutory effect upon our concert life. Early music concert audiences tend to be keen and intense. One rarely encounters the snoring scions and the gossiping *commères* who seem to be fixtures of the Friday afternoons at symphony. If the early music crowd sems to listen better and harder, it's because many of the audience practice at home the music they have come to hear onstage. Like a good restaurateur who dines out at someone else's eatery, the ticket-holder to a concert of old music is very likely to know who is in the kitchen, and how the sauce was made. This helps to keep the performer-cooks on their toes, and ensures against the drowsy routine of official concerts and hotel cuisine.

The silly side of the amateur world—krumhorn platoons, Olde Renaissance Fayres,* and all the rest—will probably be with us always. But the nonprofessional musicians who flock to their weekly rehearsals, to their weekend workshops, and to their summer early music camps are involved in something fine and life-affirming, something that transcends and disarms the satirical smirks of the outsider. For these are people who have decided to make music with and through their own bodies, rather than buying it ready-made off the shelf. In an age where everything from fried chicken to psychiatric help comes prepackaged, the decision to make one's own music oneself is perhaps only a quaintly perfumed nostalgia. But then again, maybe it is a healthy sign of rebellion and reaffirmation.

* The most successful such undertaking in my experience took place in a Medieval walled village of southern France a few years ago. The townsfolk all put on period costumes and ambled around to the music of vielles and rebecs imported for the occasion from Paris and Boston. Just as important as the costumes and the music in creating an illusion of earlier times was the temporary but total absence of automobiles.

In America, it is harder to do a Renaissance Fayre, but that doesn't stop us from trying. Absence of suitable architectural decors, and especially lack of intimate contact with the past (in Europe, they drive daily on the roads laid out by the Romans two millennia ago; they draw graffiti on Baroque statuary in public parks; and their old grannies still may insist on wearing regional costume, conceived in its essence four hundred years ago, to Sunday Mass) give our efforts to recreate Medieval or Renaissance life an involuntarily parodic aspect. On the other hand, there are Wild West Ranches in Provence, and they are just as self-evidently counterfeit as a Medieval banquet in Denver, Colorado.

XIV

Authenticity

At its most successful, Early Music does not return to the past at all but reconstructs the musical object in the here and now, enabling a new and hitherto silenced subject to speak.

—LAURENCE DREYFUS, 1983*

The performance of a piece of music can never be authentic, since music does not lend itself to being immutably fixed. More important than the antithesis "authentic-inauthentic" . . . is the point of artistic quality.

—GUSTAV LEONHARDT, 1978**

*T*HIS latter citation may have caused some surprise when it first appeared inside a record album devoted to "early instrument" performances of some well-known works. The pieces in question were Bach's Brandenburg concerti; the author of the remarks (and the director of the performances) is a man reputed to hold twice-

* "Early Music Defended against Its Devotees: A Theory of Historical Performance in the Twentieth Century," *The Musical Quarterly* (Summer 1983).
** Notes to Pro Arte record album no. L-P PAL-2022 (English translation by Robert Jordan).

daily phone conversations with Bach himself. To many musicians and music lovers these words are no more than simple good sense; but coming from someone who has spent so much time and energy researching and rethinking the performance techniques of early music (and who has such large monthly phone bills) they deserve very careful attention.

There is a radical contradiction between the claims made by many specialist performers of old music and the realities of the early music movement. As in politics, religion, and marriage, there is an important gap separating official ideology from daily practice — and it could hardly be otherwise. For the goal of "authentic" reinterpretation of music from the distant past is forever unattainable, if one defines authenticity as an exact replica of the composer's intentions or even, more modestly, as an exact reproduction of older performing techniques. But that's how the early music movement, or at any rate its purist vanguard, defines its goals.

> *A musician humbled by authenticity . . . acts willingly at the service of the composer, thereby committing himself to "truth," or, at the very least, accuracy. But there's the rub. For if we peer behind the uplifting language, we find that one attains authenticity by following the textbook rules for "scientific method." Early Music, in other words, does not preach some empathetic leap into the past in an act of imaginative* Verstehen. *What it has in mind is a strictly empirical program to verify historical practices, which, when all is said and done, are magically transformed into the composer's intentions.**

"What are you aiming for when you recreate a troubadour song from the twelfth century?" My question to the world's most eminent practitioner of Medieval music had an immediate reply: "I want to reproduce the first performance of the work as precisely as possible."

My first reaction was, suppose troubadour X had a stomachache that first night, and his performance was a flop? Maybe the second performance went much better. . . . Why this mystique of the premiere?

My reactions on succeeding days and years to that proclaimed goal

* Dreyfus, "Early Music Defended against Its Devotees."

drew me farther and farther away from that imaginary troubadour and his hypothetical digestive problems. Not that I didn't want to find out who he was or how he sang his song—it just appeared increasingly evident that reconstructing the past through the methods of factual inquiry alone was hopelessly insufficient. You might through some miracle discover exactly what dialect of Provençal was spoken in his native village; you might through an act of divine intervention discover the song manuscript with a date of first performance and copious notes about how the piece was done (don't rush to the archives just yet, young scholars; no such document has ever turned up). But you can't reproduce in your "authentic" performance his religious beliefs, his sexual preferences, his money problems, and the unfortunate effects of that too-large dinner he had unwisely ingested. You can't replicate another man's life!

During the early-to-mid-1950s there was an "authentic" revival of New Orleans jazz in this country: some of the old players were coaxed out of retirement and asked to record and to perform in public again. More than that: some young players decided to recreate the great recorded performances of the 1920s. Using the old 78s of King Oliver, of Louis Armstrong, of Jelly Roll Morton, and others (and the living example of some still-active founding fathers), the New Orleans revivalists performed and recorded interpretations that tried to be as faithful as possible in every detail to the originals.

The results? Almost uniformly disastrous. The early music practitioners of the New Orleans style had impeccable documentation to work with: far better than the scores and archival documents that are all we have from earlier centuries were the sound recordings available to the young jazzmen: recordings that replicated as no paper scratches ever can the colors and inflections of real performances.

Yet it couldn't be done. There was no way for these white, college-educated musicians to reproduce the cultural experience undergone two generations earlier by black musicians from the New Orleans ghetto. The recreations were flat, lumbering, full of good intentions, but ludicrously inept.

The forty-year time-and-culture gap was too much for the New Orleans revivalists to overcome. And the two-to-seven-century gap we face in dealing with the music of the distant past is a hundred, a thousand times more profound and insurmountable. You cannot reproduce the living music of even a few years ago, so quickly have our values and attitudes been changing. And you cannot, merely by an act of the will, hope to duplicate the aesthetic norms of any distant period. There is only one civilization we can ever hope to express completely and authentically — our own.

Still, we try, like some cheerful Sisyphus, to attain the unattainable. Over and over, we renew our attempts to recall the past, to extract its meaning and its hidden beauty. We need the strength of the past because taken all by itself our own experience is too limited, too insufficient. The present, endured in isolation from what went before, is a shallow place to be.

How precious, therefore, is the musical past as revealed to us by the early music movement. But the movement itself is, as we have seen, a very modern phenomenon. It is heavily influenced by some curious (though widely disseminated) attitudes that were born with and are proper to the machine age. Like the behavioral psychologists of the twenties, like the artificial intelligence researchers of the seventies, some early music crusaders have fallen for the ideology of scientism. Just as man is supposed to be the sum of his discrete, observable behaviors; just as thought is purported to be a series of on-and-off electrical pulses; so is historical music seen as various sets of notated pitches and codifiable performance practices. In this uniquely modern view of things, what count the most, so we are told, are data!

> The objectivity of these methods [of style analysis] invites the use of the computer, whose logic insures rigorous adherence to the criteria that have been laid down, and which can handle complex data in large quantities. For the latter reason the computer lends itself well to the systematic examination of an entire stylistic field, as in the Princeton project on the style of Josquin's music.*

One is tempted to cry "Poor Josquin des Prez!" on reading such steely prose. But it is not the long-dead Flemish master who will

* From the article "Musicology," *The New Grove's Dictionary of Music and Musicians* (London, 1980).

[93]

suffer from the implied metaphysics of the Princeton project. It is we ourselves who stand to lose. If you assume that any computer, no matter how complex, can apprehend the "entire stylistic field" that is Josquin's music, then you may be setting yourself up to overlook or ignore that which is most vital and profound in that music (or in anyone else's, for that matter).

Of course, the austere rituals of the Princeton computer lab are situated at some distance from the daily routine of the performing musician. The choirmaster rehearsing Josquin's *Missa Pange Lingua* is not likely to share many concerns with that big calculating machine in New Jersey. Still, the values of contemporary musicology (a field of study unknown in fifteenth-century Flanders) may insinuate themselves one way or another into his choir's performance. When those values translate into respect for the musical text and careful attention to our current knowledge of Renaissance musical style and practices, we stand to gain both in understanding and in musical pleasure. When such values manifest themselves as reticence, pallid expression, and a reluctance to make controversial decisions, we stand to come out with the short end of the stick.

A performing musician, if he is to succeed, must still center his work in a place that lies outside the realm of the scientifically knowable, of the computer program and the scholarly monograph. What is known as fact (and what isn't known, as well) must be reimagined by the interpretive artist if the dead work he is charged with resuscitating is to start breathing again. Without a large dose of humility about the limits of our knowledge, and without a goodly measure of affectionate empathy, our efforts to recreate the past will come to naught.

"Obscurantist!" I can hear the cry already, resonating down the corridors of some specialist journal's office space. Please forbear; I am not trying to bring back the bad old days. I make no case for the thumping pianist, the megalomaniac conductor, or the glass-shattering concert soprano. Those people will survive very well without this book to defend them. I mean to make a case *en famille,* among people who already know and love the sounds of old instruments and the expressive power of early performance techniques.

Our devotion to the music of the distant past has led us to serve it better through knowledge of its proper historical context. To complete that context, to fill in the gaps that mere knowledge cannot complete, we must call forth the same effort of creative imagination that is contained in the musical works themselves. As in politics, religion, and marriage, that means learning to live with a certain number of contradictions, and assuming a certain number of risks. It means accepting a limited degree of success as the best deal possible under the circumstances. It also helps to keep a sense of humor through it all, lest we become relentless Captain Ahabs pursuing some elusive white whale of authenticity, and losing a measure of our humanity in the process.

We performers need the discipline of scholarship. We need the tools of modern research, and we need the results those tools have obtained for us. What we *don't* need is the mind-set of the technocratic priesthood. There are dimensions of any artistic activity that cannot be harnessed to the yoke of scientific cognition. Those dimensions are just as important for Campra as for Chopin; just as necessary for Monteverdi as for Mahler. The tigers of wrath are wiser than the horses of instruction!

XV

Conclusions; Does the Past have a Future?

*T*HE pioneers of the early music movement worked by and large in isolation from the musical establishment. In part, this was a matter of choice; one might not want to belong to the "big world" of concert life. For many a recorder player, gambist, or teacher of country dances there was a certain comfort and even congeniality to be found by living in the margins.

From the first, early music has found a warm welcome among those who for one reason or another maintain a certain critical distance from the social mainstream. Sometimes the artists and writers, the nuclear physicists and macrobiologists who like the music of the distant past are more supportive of the unusual repertoire and the offbeat tone colors than the professional musician caste itself.

> . . . *On the night of the concert (19 December 1891) the studio was packed. The best-known progressives in London had turned out for the occasion — artists, poets, writers: they were fascinated by this little Frenchman whose very appearance was more pre-Raphaelite than the pre-Raphaelites themselves with velvet suit, lace ruffles and silver buckles on his shoes. His music recaptured for them the delights of a lost enchantment: the embodiment of all*

*their aspirations. He was loved on sight and when the concert was over they applauded uproariously. At last Dolmetsch had found his audience.**

Until recently, in fact, the audience for early music had not changed much in kind since those Bloomsbury days. The mainstream music lovers shunned the early music milieu for both good reasons and bad. On the one hand, there was the intellectual laziness and profound incuriosity that often afflict people with conservative tastes (bad reason). On the other hand, there was an incontrovertible fact: those early efforts to do early music were often inept and fumbling affairs (possible good reason). Why undergo voluntary punishment when life is already full of the other, obligatory kind?

Illustrations were also played by Mr. Galpin [the founder of modern organology] on the Recorder . . . and the original of the cornet, a straight conical tube, with lateral holes. The effect of Ein Feste Burg *played on the latter instrument, and accompanied on the Regal, is indescribable, and fully accounts for our ancestors' partiality for instruments of the string family.***

Thus the critic of the *Musical World* writing for the Londoners of 1890; his disdain for the goings-on of musical antiquarians has been shared by countless reviewers in the decades since.

It can be assumed, then, that both performers and audiences in those pioneering years were often less well trained, less musically aware, than their counterparts in the center of concert life. Even as standards of professionalism and sophistication have grown higher, some of this pre-Raphaelite heritage lingers on. Many an early music player has come to the field from literature, history, or another art form. In the conservatories that support early music programs the typical student tends to have a better liberal arts background than his buddy across the corridor in the trombone department; but the early

---

* Margaret Campbell, *Dolmetsch: The Man and His Work* (Seattle, 1975), p. 41.
** Quoted in Campbell, *Dolmetsch,* p. 25.

music student may have more than average trouble in sight-reading or transposition or rapid passage work. The trombone player, on the other hand, has never heard of Petrarch. But it is likely that he can and does play with great proficiency.

In the audience, too, one finds a disproportionate number of literati and visual artists. From William Morris and George Bernard Shaw to Ezra Pound to John Hollander and W. D. Snodgrass, the writers have provided the players with a steady chorus of encouragement and approval. Many, too, are the painters and sculptors who splash, hack, and chop their way toward immortality, to the recorded strains of Susato or Scarlatti. Not that loving poetry or painting makes you a bad listener. On the contrary, it may enable you to focus on the music most effectively. There is no denying, however, the seductive charm of historical association. People have been drawn to early music because of its sound and substance; they have also come by to catch a quick whiff of the dear dead days.

The picturesque, the quaint, and the anecdotal sides of the early music world constituted much of the movement's appeal at the beginning; and they are still-present dimensions of the repertoire's continuing charm. In America especially, the Dolmetsch ethos has reemerged with a new intensity. The fin-de-siècle lotus-eating of the first years has been wedded to the no-nonsense business of hard sell. Walter Pater has gone to graduate school, and he has come forth with an MBA in marketing:

> "Four brand new and exciting programs — saluting five centuries of great Italian music and the seven colorful and historic cities in which it flourished . . . at the courts of the Medici, Sforzas, and Gonzagas . . . under Brunelleschi's fantastic dome for Santa Maria del Fiore or Michelangelo's glorious ceiling for the Sistine Chapel . . . in the mosaic vastness of San Marco, the gilded palazzi along the Grand Canal and the jewel-box theatre of La Fenice. 10 Brilliantly Gifted Solo Singers and Players, 50 Medieval, Renaissance and Baroque instruments, including viola da gamba — vielle — nun's fiddle — rebec — lute — vihuela — theorbo — sackbut — gemshorn — cornetto — oud — shawm

— rauschpfeife — citole — dulcian — psaltery . . . subscribe NOW and avoid disappointment." *

Easy it may be to mock the nostalgic side of the early music movement, especially when nostalgia is packaged like Wheaties. It seems, though, that the longing for a calmer, simpler Golden Age lies deep within us. The backward-turning side of Olde Musicke has been roundly condemned by the staunchest of the modernists; yet that is a relatively harmless neurosis compared with the truly awesome spiritual disorders of the machine age, such as the theater organ and the MX missile.

Let's face it, though: the early music scene is changing. The dulcimer-strumming flower children have been overtaken by a newer generation of trained professionals. It is no longer enough to dress in ruffles and to brandish thirty odd-shaped musical objects at the public; people can now hear those instruments played well, by men and women in street clothes. The musicians' skills are greater than before, the audience's expectations are higher. And the early music movement is inching, slowly but perceptibly, back into the fold of the concert mainstream.

Is this newly won acceptance of early music such good news? In those earlier decades, the performers and the performances of old music suffered from chronic neglect by the general public. Now the tides of fashion have turned. Leonhardt will never outdraw Pavarotti, but he has a significant place in the musical sun. Monteverdi still sells fewer tickets than plain vanilla Verdi, but the former's box-office receipts are nonetheless healthy and still growing.

Will success spoil Sigismondo d'India? Although there's nothing especially ennobling about poverty and neglect, there was a kind of purity about the movement in its early years, a desire to find the right musical solution for its own sake, regardless of the opinions reigning in the world outside. This commitment to high standards, coupled

* Quoted in Laurence Dreyfus, "Early Music Defended against Its Devotees: A Theory of Historical Performance in the Twentieth Century," *The Musical Quarterly* (Summer 1983).

with a rapidly improving level of technical proficiency, makes the early music field still a bracing and invigorating place to be. Rarely does one find such sincerity and dedication in the commercial concert circuit.

Ethical standards remain high — but temptation is knocking at the door. The blandishments of impresarios and record companies, hungry for new product, may go far toward turning what was once daring and adventuresome into the humdrum routine of concerts-as-usual. In the now plethoric discography of the early music movement, there are more than a few recordings that betray hasty decision-making and insufficient rehearsal. Recent seasons have seen more than their share of indifferent live performances, put together perhaps because there was a public ready, willing, and able to pay the price of admission.

The marketplace has already begun to reshape parts of the movement. The current rapprochement of early music performance with the academy — universities and conservatories — may also, as we have said, deprive this once-kinky endeavor of its original daring and spunk. Then, too, we are living in the 1980s. Bloomsbury is now a grimy London neighborhood of cheap hotels for American tourists; and the revolutionary slogans of the sixties are currently as *démodé* as the Hula-Hoop and the CB radio. We live once again in a cautious, conservative time, and our performances of early music, inevitably, are going to be the reflection of our own, present-day state of mind.

Attribute it to the *Zeitgeist* or to something else if you will — in any case, the blandness syndrome is an observable, describable component of early music life. We can all recall readings of important music, be it Beethoven or Byrd, in which everything seemed to be in place, but where some level of deeper engagement seemed to be lacking. The too-careful, insufficiently felt-through interpretation can occur anywhere in our modern concert world; but it is especially an occupational hazard in the early music field.

The aesthetic conflicts within the early music movement echo the greater struggles in the world outside. Does the movement repose essentially on old rules and regulations, or is it, in the words of gambist-scholar Laurence Dreyfus, "an inimitable antistyle"? Do we strive above all for objective knowledge about the old music we play, or do we seek to recreate its inner experience? Who's the god of early music — is he Apollo or is he Dionysus?

Perhaps, after all, we don't need a god for this particular activity. To each performer is given the crucial task of reconciling heart and head. Every interpreter of early music is like the condemned man in the Hasidic parable: the man's punishment, for whatever crime he had committed, was to walk a tightrope across a vast chasm. Somehow, miraculously, he negotiated the crossing, and his life was thus spared.

"How did you do it?" asked an anxious onlooker.

"When I felt myself slipping off to the right side," came the reply, "I leaned a little more to the left. When I felt myself sliding off toward the left, I leaned over to the right."

Performing Landini or Lassus, Tartini or Telemann; playing any music whatsoever from the distant past involves a similar kind of balancing act. The feat may seem impossible. It may seem to demand superhuman powers of skill and coordination. A few of our colleagues have nonetheless managed to do it. They have crossed the chasm unscathed.

The successful acrobat amuses the spectators and saves his own neck. The rewards for negotiating the early music tightrope include the above-named perks; but there are even better reasons for venturing across the chasm of the distant past. We need the music of our ancestors. We need its calm and its passion, its sensuality and its grace. We need the opportunity this music affords us to come face to face with remote yet vitally important parts of our own selves.

Does early music have a future? All external signs point to its continued success and acceptance. Former organetto players now conduct major symphony orchestras; cocktail-party chatter now turns to the merits and demerits of Baroque opera when the talk of real estate begins to sag; and the FM band of our radio, despite the protests of Doctor Zwang, seems firmly committed to Vivaldi for breakfast at old Baroque pitch. Despite such worldly triumphs, the early music fraternity may be in trouble. As we have seen, some of the forces that first brought the movement into being are showing signs of fatigue. The music is still there, unyielding in its quiet truthfulness. But the human context that made it possible to discover those works afresh is changing rapidly.

Early music needs constant renewal to live. Will the music, its sound and its sense, continue to be rethought in vital, meaningful ways? Will the performers continue to grow and to search out the best solutions, the finest challenges? Let us so hope; we need the past to keep our souls in balance. Strike the viol! Touch the lute! Wake the harp! Inspire the flute! And man those tightropes!

And Now
the Players

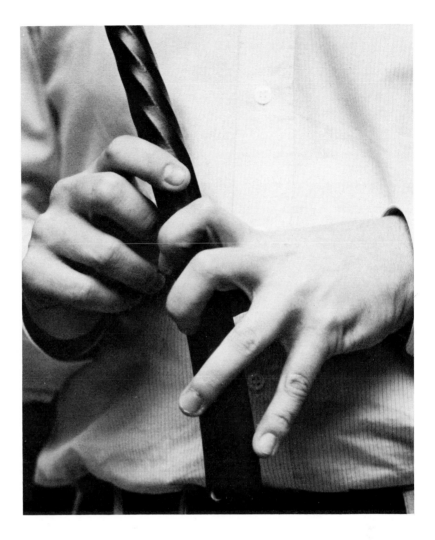

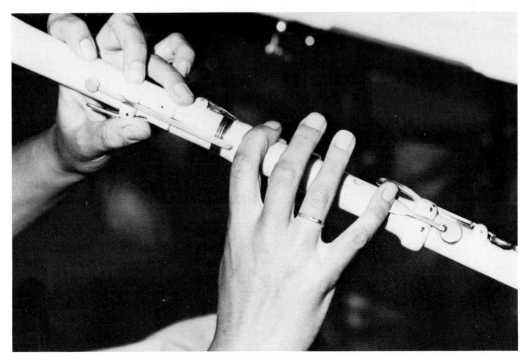

*Bass Dirk Snellings sings a Gregorian antiphon
during a concert of the Belgian-based Huelgas
Ensemble. The setting is the Pieterskerk in Utrecht,
the Netherlands.*

*Paul van Nevel directs the Huelgas Ensemble in a
performance of music from fourteenth-century
Cyprus. The complex polyphony of these motets,
based on Gregorian chant, offered a challenge to the
ear in the Pieterskerk's "wet" acoustic. Van Nevel's
densely orchestrated versions were themselves a
source of discussion and controversy.*

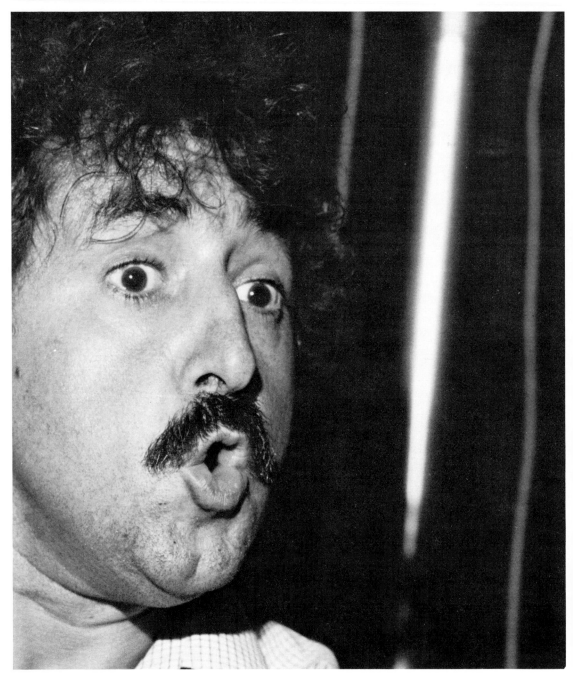

Paul van Nevel

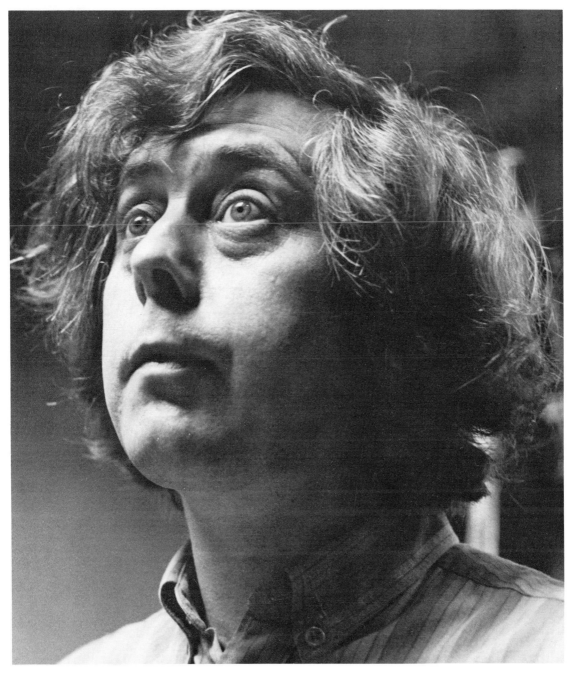

Anthony Rooley, leader of the London Consort of Musicke, was always aware of the camera's presence but never allowed that intrusion to get in the way of his BBC recording session. He, soprano Emma Kirkby, and the other singers who comprise the Consort had finished a tour of Portugal that morning and were scheduled to leave the next morning for Italy. They had a scant eight hours to look over and sing unfamiliar Italian madrigals by seventeenth-century composer Girolamo Frescobaldi.

Evelyn Tubb joins Emma Kirkby and Anthony Rooley during the Frescobaldi recording session at a small London church in the shadow of St. Paul's Cathedral. The Consort of Musicke's repertoire is primarily vocal — madrigals and lute songs from the sixteenth and early seventeenth centuries.

The coffee line brings together the early music performers and construction workers.

Emma Kirkby

Sterling Jones

Pan, an ensemble that specializes in music of the
Ars Nova (fourteenth-century works from Italy and
France, representing some of the most subtle,
difficult, and challenging repertoire of any time or
place), awaits the moment to perform in an unlikely
setting — an elementary-school gym in Cambridge,
Massachusetts.

The group's vielle player, Sterling Jones, currently
teaching at the Schola Cantorum in Basel, was a
charter member of the celebrated Studio der Fruehen

Musik; in collaboration with Studio's leader,
Thomas Binkley, Jones evolved a way of performing
on Medieval stringed instruments that went far
beyond anything previously attempted. Jones's
experiments with the expressive potential of the
vielle and the rebec have made a permanent
contribution to our understanding of Medieval
performing styles. (See Chapter VI for more on
Binkley and Jones.)

Singers Barbara Thornton and Ben Bagby of the
Sequentia ensemble rehearsing for an important
Boston concert. Even under such pressure they and
the third member of this ensemble, Margrit
Tindemans, who plays vielle, were responsive to the
requirements of the camera. Bagby and Thornton
founded the ensemble on completing their studies in
Basel with the Studio der Fruehen Musik.
Inevitably, Sequentia's way with Medieval monody
has often been compared with the style of the
pioneering Studio, but Sequentia has succeeded in
staking out its own ground and creating its own
musical profile. Sequentia's sober, uncompromising
performances of twelfth- and thirteenth-century
music have something in them of the earnestness of
our own decade; not unsurprisingly, these musicians
have a special flair for the musical (and literary)
ethos of the students and clerics who flocked to the
Sorbonne six hundred years ago.

Countertenors Ken Fitch and Fred
Raffensperger of the Boston Camerata
conspire to overthrow the prophet Daniel
in the Camerata's 1983 production of
Ludus Danielis (Play of Daniel). *Andrea
von Ramm, whose work is discussed in
Chapter XII, sang the role of Daniel and,
doubling as stage director, sought to point
this Medieval French work (circa 1200)
back to its biblical roots; the staging,
costumes, and set design made extensive
use of motifs from ancient Persian and
Babylonian art.*

Nancy Armstrong (left) as the queen in the Play of
Daniel. *Carol Pharo (above) was the choreographer
and principal dancer in the production.*

Paul O'Dette and Lyle Norstrom performing the only surviving work "for two to play on one Lute" — a galliard by composer and lutenist John Dowland (1563 – 1626). O'Dette directs the Musicians of Swanne Alley, a Renaissance consort in New York City, and has quickly established himself as one of the most gifted virtuoso technicians on an instrument noted for its ornery intractability.

Lutenist James Tyler here teams up with jazz musician Ted Curson. Tyler, now director of the London Early Music Group, was once with Noah Greenberg's New York Pro Musica (see Chapter V) and David Munrow's Early Music Consort of London (see Chapter IV). All our paths crossed by chance in a Boston hotel lobby. The encounter produced an unusual photographic opportunity and an unusual musical product as well; the Renaissance passamezzo moderno *ground bass (considered by some scholars to be a distant ancestor of the blues), which Tyler began strumming, became the basis for several eloquent choruses by Curson on the piccolo trumpet.*

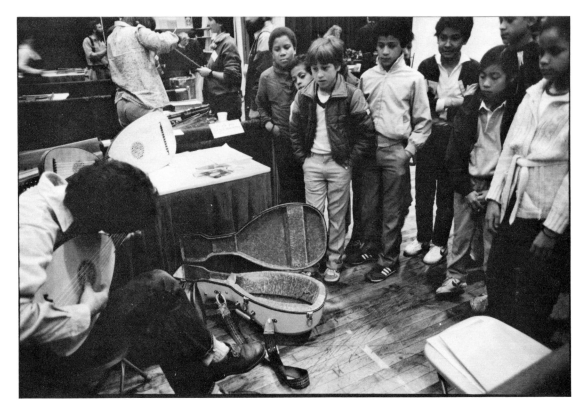

A Christmas card to Diana Poulton by Giovanni Pellini, an Italian friend, who for years superimposed his face on images of long-ago lute players.

A lutenist trying out a new instrument under the gaze of Boston school children at the second Boston Early Music Festival.

A group of children listening to a lute player would be a welcome sight for Diana Poulton. Here in her London home she and lutenist Christopher Wilson review material to be published by the Lute Society in commemoration of her eightieth birthday. Diana Poulton's many contributions to the modern rebirth of the lute include a biography and critical edition of the great Elizabethan lutenist John Dowland and the first instruction manual for the Renaissance lute since the sixteenth century!

Lutenist Joel Cohen at a rehearsal of the Boston Camerata.

The hand of Nigel North.

Michael Jaffee, director of New York's very active
Waverly Consort, practices in his apartment on
Manhattan's Upper West Side.

Waverly co-director Kay Jaffee (above right) and bowed-string player Rosamund Morley during a dress rehearsal of the ensemble's Medieval Christmas pageant at New England Conservatory's Jordan Hall. The Waverly Consort performs primarily Medieval and Renaissance music.

Bass David Thomas has sung with just about every English early music ensemble imaginable, in repertoire ranging from the twelfth to the early nineteenth century (see Chapter XII). His unusual ability to sing well in every range from basso profundo to head-voice tenor and his vigorous and enthusiastic musical personality have helped make

*his one of the most recorded male voices of the
twentieth century. His surroundings and his many
interests outside of music contrast with the very
rarefied and specialized world of his musical activity,
and seem to give him the necessary breathing space
for his busy career.*

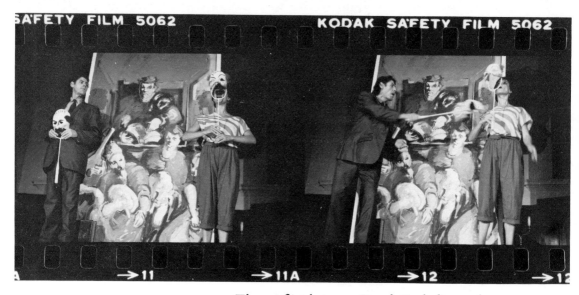

The conflict between Dutch Catholics and Protestants during the Reformation was the basis for a lively, intense, and often funny evening of music theater by the Dutch group Camerata Trajectina. Combining theological polemics, native popular tunes of the sixteenth century, and a large dose of counterculture satire, The Whore of Babylon, *performed late at night at a little church in Utrecht, had the audience jumping to their feet at the evening's end.*

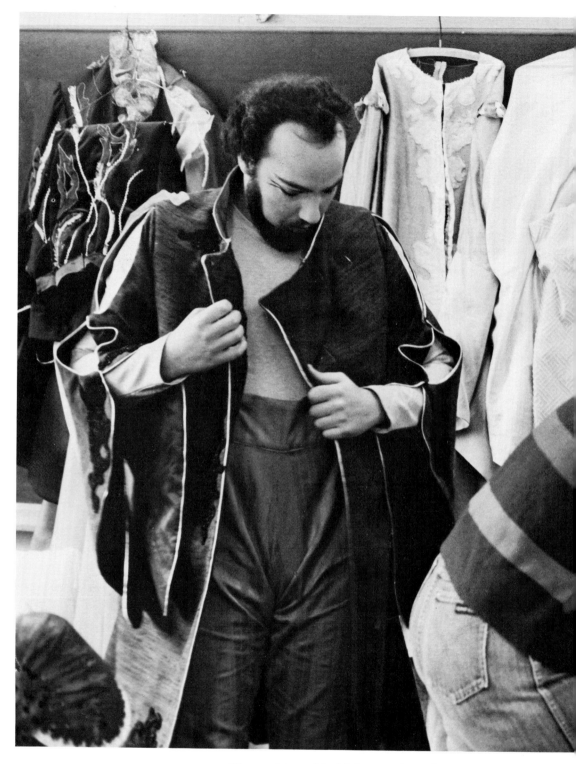

*Singers James Maddelena and Sanford Sylvan
preparing for their roles as Abramane and Zopiera
in the American premiere of Jean-Philippe Rameau's
opera Zoroastre. This 1983 production by the
Banchetto Musicale, a Boston group specializing in*

*Baroque performance, was among the many events
in both Europe and the United States
commemorating the composer's three hundredth
birthday anniversary.*

French singer Sophie Boulin as Amélite, the lover of Zoroastre, and American Nancy Armstrong as Erinice, the ally of Abramane and arch-enemy of Amélite, performing in Zoroastre.

Tenor Nigel Rogers and countertenor James Bowman, both from London, were photographed there: Rogers in Queen Victoria's Gardens and Bowman in the Covent Garden area.

Rogers's special feeling for the virtuoso vocal music of the early Baroque has been amply

documented on recordings (see also Chapters VI and XII); similarly, Bowman's many recorded performances (with, among others, the late David Munrow) have made his distinctive falsettist timbre familiar all over Western Europe and America.

During the 1983 Utrecht festival cornettist Bruce Dickey and sackbut player Charles Toet appeared in a concert with the Netherlands Kamerkoor. Dickey

also coached a number of aspiring cornetto players during a morning workshop.

Simon Standage is one of Europe's outstanding Baroque violinists and, like many of his English colleagues, an immensely versatile performer. His clean, accurate playing has helped to shape hundreds of recordings and concert performances. He is concertmaster of Trevor Pinnock's English Consort, and first violinist of the Salomon Quartet, both based in London. Many English and American ensembles employ the same nucleus of skilled players under different ensemble names: Standage has been present as section leader of almost every currently prominent English ensemble. An intense person, he has a charming, if infrequent, smile, and a wry sense of humor.

Michael Morrow (left), now in semi-retirement, founded the pioneering ensemble Musica Reservata together with John Beckett, who declined to be photographed for this book.

Musica Reservata, which flourished in the late sixties and early seventies, featured the extraordinary singing voice of American mezzo Jantina Noorman. The ensemble's experiments in vocal style (Noorman could sound like a dying princess or a fishwife, depending on the context) were controversial at the time. Some of the group's most daring innovations, such as vibratoless singing, are now taken for granted in current performances of Medieval and Renaissance music.

Trevor Pinnock is playing a 1770 Shudi and Broadwood harpsichord at Fenton House, London, where he is head of the music committee charged with preserving an extensive collection of musical

instruments. Pinnock's passionate, fiery harpsichord
style rapidly gained him a wide audience. His strong
musical ideas are equally evident in the
performances he directs with the English Consort.

London, a sophisticated and dynamic city, still has room for a nineteenth-century knife sharpener. At once forward-moving and respectful of the past, London is one of the major centers for early music.

Boston Early Music Festival, 1983

A town crier announces the beginning of the second Boston Early Music Festival, an event that drew 8,000 people from all over the world. The Festival's tone in 1983 tended to be earnest rather than celebratory.

Gustav Leonhardt at one of the many Boston Early Music Festival workshops illustrates a fine point of Orlando Gibbons's keyboard music through a

judicious use of body Dutch. (Leonhardt's
considerable contributions to early music are
discussed in Chapter XI.)

Organist Luigi-Ferdinando Tagliavini, who performed at the 1983 Boston Early Music Festival, is one of the few Italian musicians to have made an important contribution to the world of early music performance.

The uniquely gifted Ralph Dopmeyer, owner, producer, and driving force behind Titanic Records, has his recording business on Rice Street in Cambridge, Massachusetts, where he can be found most of the time sipping coffee or exotic wines amidst an array of electronic equipment, papers, and other paraphernalia.

*Two visitors to the Boston Early Music Festival try
out a reproduction of a Medieval vielle. In the lower
left-hand corner is a modern version of a sixteenth-
century Spanish* vihuela da mano.

*German-born Friedrich von Huene learned to make
modern flutes at the Powell Workshop in Boston
before many requests for Baroque flutes led him to
manufacture historical woodwinds — recorders and
wooden transverse flutes. Many of the younger
instrument makers received their training at von
Huene's Brookline, Massachusetts, workshop.*

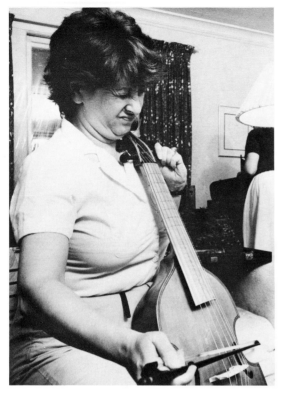

Flautist Mark Hopkins seems to need some help in finding his place as he, Phyllis Klein, Tom Kurz, and Sybil Kevy play at their weekly get-togethers, a scene replicated throughout the world by other amateur consorts interested in keeping early music alive and well.

Caitlin Phillips joins Larry Zukof and Sasha Wizansky.

Larry Zukof, director of the Brookline, Massachusetts, Music School, and a member of the Boston Camerata as both player and singer, in an outdoor rehearsal with his students on a long, hot day in July. From left to right: Jessica Hamlin, Caitlin Riley, Sasha Wizansky, Katie Zukof with the great bass recorder, and Neva Hicks with the violin.

*New York – based musician Steve Silverstein
manufactures and performs on historical
woodwinds. Pictured here at the 1983 Boston Early
Music Festival, he is testing another instrument
maker's dulcian.*

*Roy Sansom, a member of the Boston-based
Greenwood Consort, can perform on krumhorn,
recorder, rackett, Renaissance harp, pipe, and tabor.
The Consort specializes in fifteenth- and sixteenth-
century music.*

Utrecht Early Music Festival, 1983

Last-minute schedule changes for the Utrecht festival were hand-lettered on a poster. Concerts were scheduled daily at 10:30 a.m., 11:00 a.m., 11:30 a.m., 12:45 p.m., 2:00 p.m., 2:30 p.m., 3:15 p.m., 3:30 p.m., 4:00 p.m., 5:00 p.m., 7:00 p.m., 8:15 p.m., 10:15 p.m., and finally 11:00 p.m. Even two enthusiastic reporters couldn't cover all the events.

Festivals are times of celebration, anticipation,
excitement, for the musicians as well as for the
audiences. In an empty auditorium, harpsichordist
John Gibbons works alone, readying his instrument
for the Boston Museum Trio's Utrecht debut.

English bass-baritone Paul Hillier directs a rehearsal of the Hilliard Ensemble in the Saint Matthew Passion *by seventeenth-century composer Heinrich*

*Schütz. Tenor Rogers Covey-Crump (far left), active
in many English ensembles, sings the role of the
Evangelist in the Schütz work.*

*Still near the beginning of his career,
Reinhard Goebel has quickly risen to
stardom on the basis of a stunning,
flawless Baroque violin technique.
His colleagues in the Musica Antiqua
Köln (Cologne, West Germany) —
harpsichordist Andreas Staier, violist
Karlheinz Steeb, and American cellist
Phoebe Carrai — rehearse with Goebel
for their Utrecht performances. Not
shown is violinist Hajo Bäss.*

Belgian choral conductor Philippe Herreweghe directs vocal ensembles in Ghent, Belgium (the Collegium Vocale), and in Paris (the Chapelle Royale). His performances frequently involve collaborations with outstanding European early instrument specialists.

In a milieu dominated by Northern European and Anglo-Saxon players, Catalan gambist Jordi Savall contributes an important measure of Mediterranean brio and temperament. Active as a soloist, he also directs the ensemble Hesperion XX in repertoire ranging from the Middle Ages to the late Baroque.

Concert's end at Utrecht brought a touching and
appropriate gesture from conductor Herreweghe: he
shares applause and flowers with one of the unsung
heroines of the early music movement, Baroque
violinist Janine Rubinlicht.

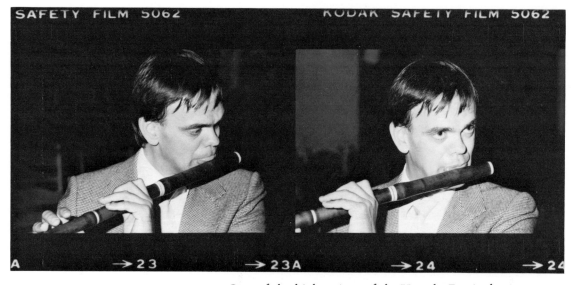

One of the high points of the Utrecht Festival was an appearance by the Kuijken brothers: Bart (above), Sigiswald (right), and Wieland (following page). An 11:00 p.m. concert of Haydn trios drew a thousand people to a little Romanesque church in Utrecht. (See also Chapter IX.)

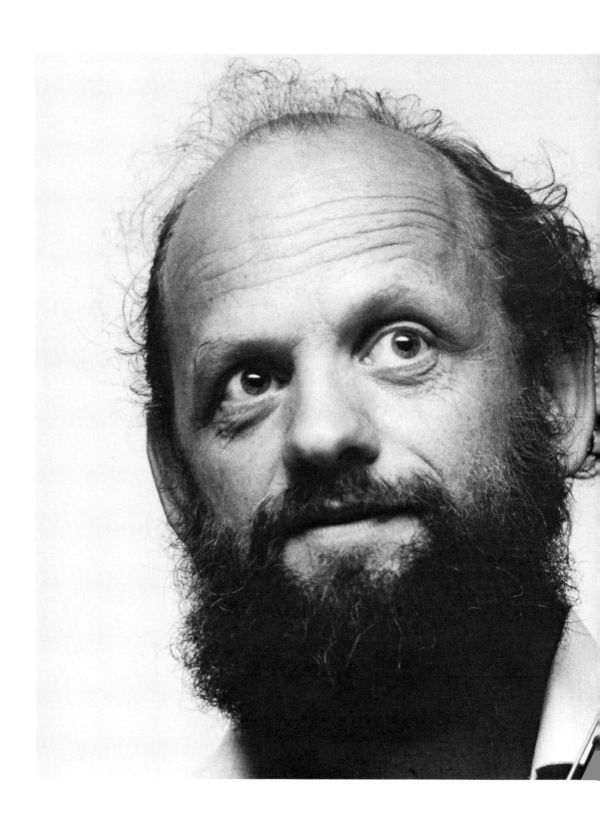

Michel Henry, oboist with the Amsterdam Baroque Orchestra, in rehearsal for Handel's Messiah, *the concluding work of the 1983 Utrecht Festival.*

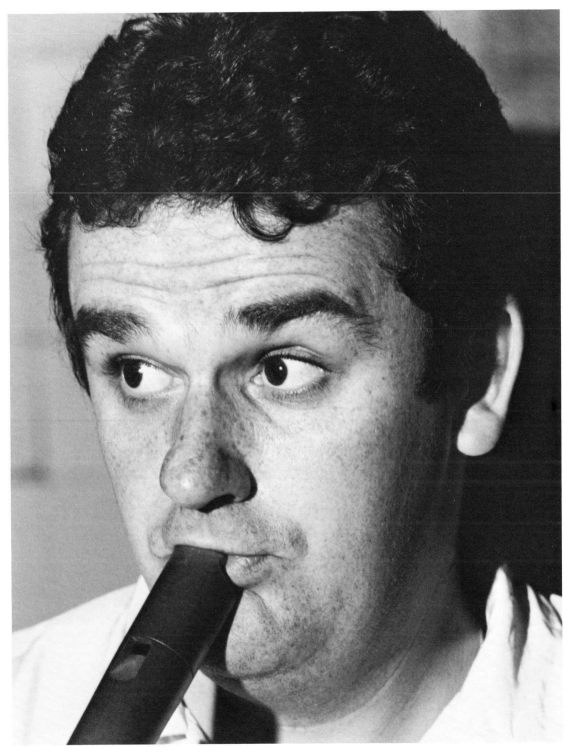

Peter Hannan, recorder player with Vancouver-based Hortulani Musicae, the only Canadian ensemble present at the Utrecht Festival. Other members are lutenist Ray Nurse, singer Nan Mackie, and gambist Erica Northcott.

LEFT: These Baroque and Renaissance-style recorders belong to the Amsterdam-based Loeki Stardust Quartet.

BELOW: The noontime performance of Loeki Stardust concluded unexpectedly with an arrangement for four recorders of the theme from The Pink Panther. *These four young players, Bertho Driever, Karel van Steenhover, Paul Leenhouts, and Daniël Brüggen, abjure the heavy protocol of concert-hall tradition; their obvious pleasure in creating a mild scandal from time to time does not interfere for a moment with their superb sense of ensemble work.*

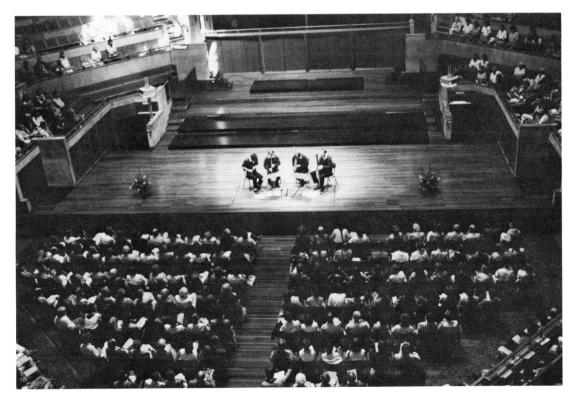

Belgian countertenor René Jacobs, one of the busiest early music singers on the Continent, is rehearsing here with Concerto Vocale (including soprano Judith Nelson, lutenist Konrad Junghaenel, and harpsichordist William Christie).

Nicolas Papp, American-born but now a resident of
Amsterdam, is convinced that early Baroque bassists
played the instrument this way. "Look at
Veronese's painting Marriage at Cana. You will see

the instruments in this position," he explained.
Perhaps those musicians, too — like him — were only
playing around and were caught by the "journalist"
of the day.

Anner Bylsma recording far into the night for
Titanic Records. At 10:30 *p.m. he was through only*
two Frescobaldi canzone *out of the planned five*
pieces.

Bylsma and his colleague John Gibbons were a tired duo a couple of days later, when they were joined by Frans Brüggen for a Boston concert. Bylsma is to the Baroque cello what Charlie Parker was to the alto saxophone: a constant source of awe and emulation to others in the same line of business.

Daniel Stepner, concertmaster, and Martin Pearlman, harpsichordist and musical director of Boston's Banchetto Musicale, rehearse Vivaldi's Four Seasons, *performed that day at the De Cordova Museum in Lincoln, Massachusetts.*

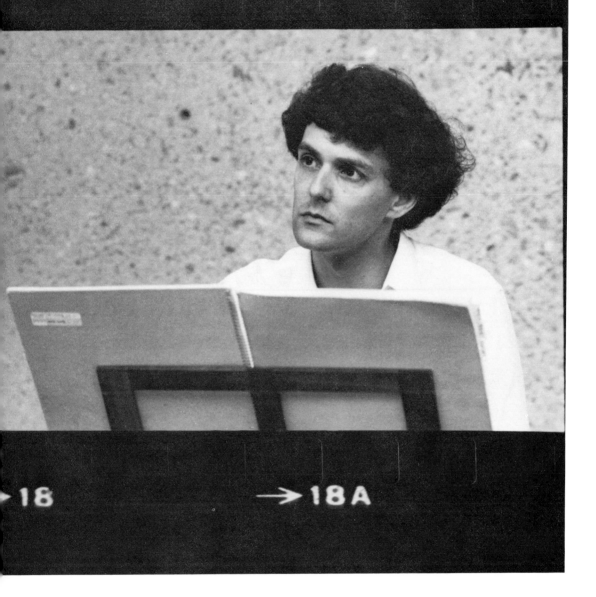

LEFT: At the same performance soprano Sharon Baker sang Vivaldi's motet "O que coeli." Horn soloist Jean Rife prepares a Mozart concerto for the concert.

RIGHT: A rehearsal break finds cellist Shannon Snapp, bassist Tom Coleman, and violinist Steve Martin discussing the cost of replacing a cello — not a small amount, since the cost of a first-rate instrument goes higher each year.

San Franciscan Elizabeth Legvin, a member of the Aston Magna Orchestra, and Myron Lutzke of New York's Aulos Ensemble.

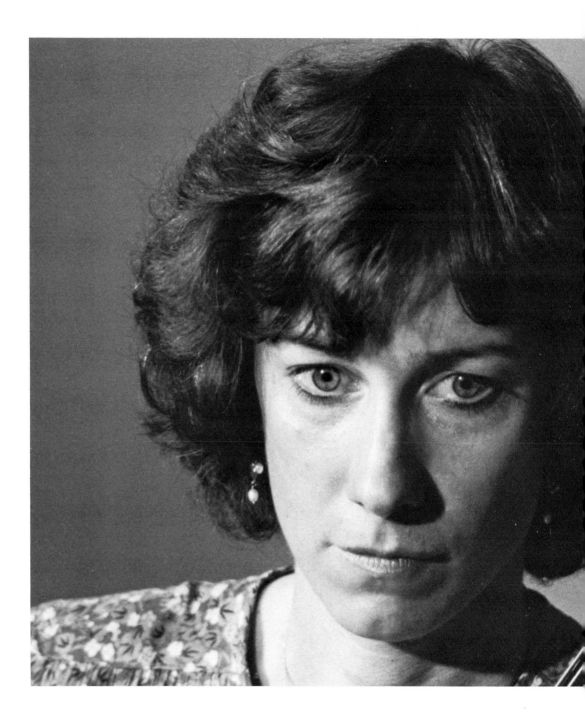

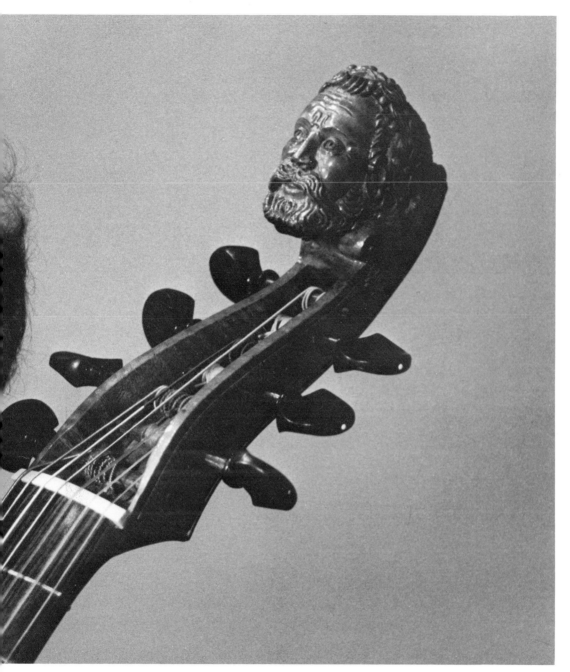

Gambist Laura Jeppesen is one of Wieland Kuijken's outstanding American students. She appears regularly in this country with the Boston Museum Trio and the Boston Camerata (where she is a frequent performer as well on the Medieval vielle).

LEFT: Albert Fuller relaxes during a break in rehearsal of his Aston Magna Orchestra, an experiment in what would happen if a group of scholars, musicians, interested participants, and observers came together for a month's residency in the Berkshire Mountains — a climate where ideas and music centered around a single theme would be discussed and played.

RIGHT: Anthony Martin appears as a soloist or featured performer with many American groups. He is also a member of Brüggen's orchestra.

The Boston Museum Trio (Laura Jeppesen, John Gibbons, and Daniel Stepner) in rehearsal with Indiana-based Baroque violinist Stanley Richie for their performance at the Boston Museum of Fine Arts. All the musicians of the trio also perform in Europe, as members of Frans Brüggen's Orchestra of the Eighteenth Century. (Brüggen and his orchestra are discussed in Chapter X.)

Jaap Schroeder and Lawrence McDonald, in Great Barrington, Massachusetts, rehearse Mozart's Quintet in A Major. Schroeder's expertise in string playing of the Mozart-Haydn period makes him one of the most traveled performers in the early music

→ 33   → 33A

field. His sure musicianship and keen interpretive insight have graced ensembles in his native Netherlands and in Switzerland, England, and the United States.

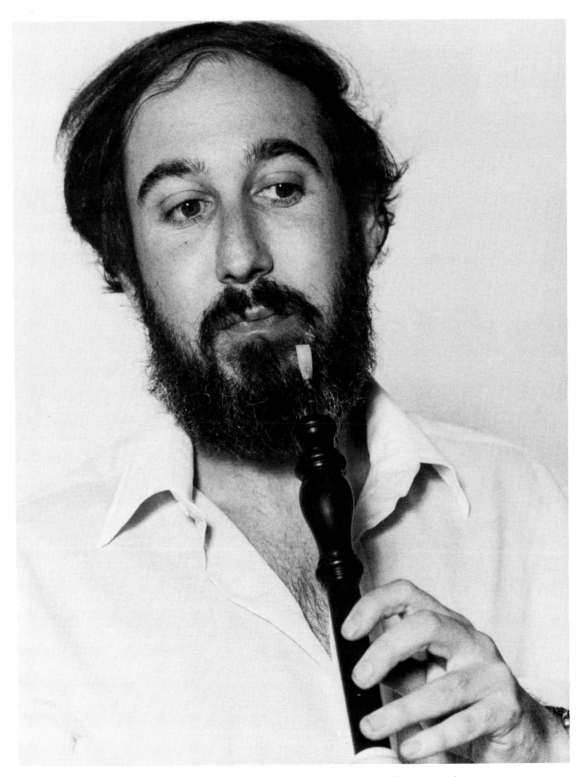

Two young American specialists in early woodwinds, Marc Schachtman and Robin Howell. Oboist Schachtman leads the New York – based

Baroque violinist Jane Starkman, the newly named concertmistress of the Philadelphia Baroque Orchestra.

Aulos ensemble, and Basel-trained Howell freelances all over the country on practically every instrument imaginable.

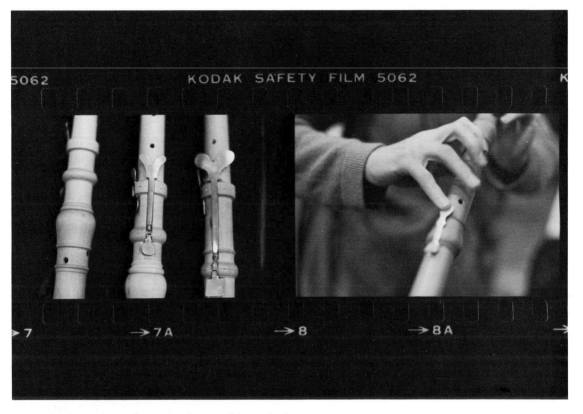

An experienced pro, and one of America's outstanding modern flautists, John Solum (left) has brought his savvy and expertise to the rapidly evolving world of early instrument performance.

Ton Koopman directs the Amsterdam Baroque Orchestra, soloists, and an English chorus, The Sixteen, in a performance of Handel's Messiah. Koopman's sense of phrase and musical pulse, while derived from early performance treatises, is highly personal. He coached the English chorus into patterns of articulation that differed markedly from most people's expectations of this repertoire.

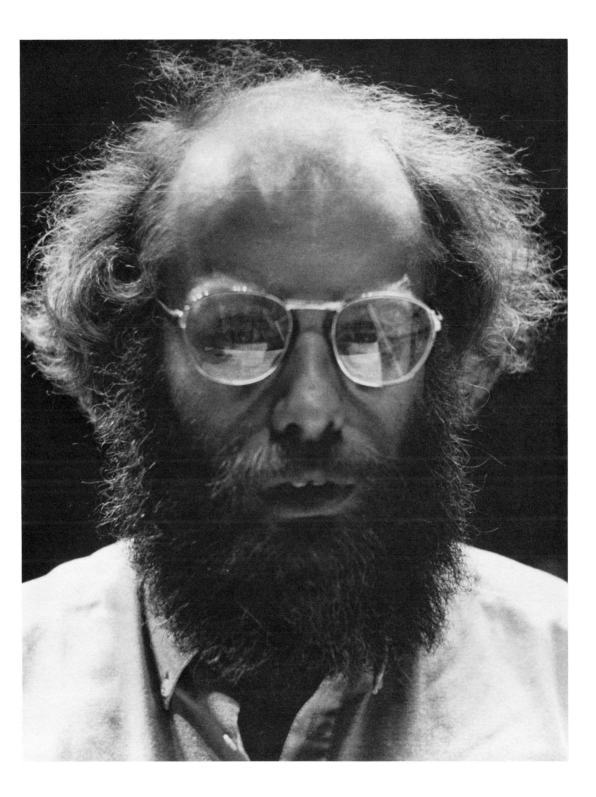

At a BBC afternoon recording session in London's
magnificent Saint John's Smith Square, Roger
Norrington directed the Schutz Choir of London;
the London Classical Players, a large orchestra of
period instruments; and fortepianist Melvin Tan in

Beethoven's Choral Fantasia. *That evening the capacity audience rewarded this performance with a standing ovation; the early music movement is well on its way to colonizing the nineteenth century!*

*Frans Brüggen rehearses his
Orchestra of the Eighteenth
Century for a Utrecht performance.
Concertmistress Lucy van Dael's
musical presence helps give the
string section its shape and color.*

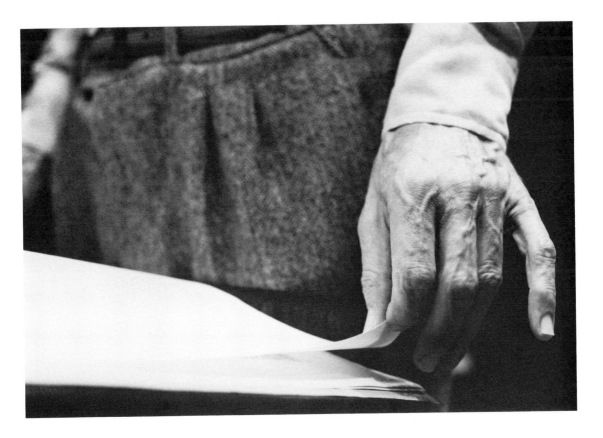

*Christopher Hogwood conducts the Boston
Symphony Orchestra during the 1983 Tanglewood
Festival season. In the same year, he went on to
conduct modern orchestras in St. Louis, San*

Francisco, and Detroit. Hogwood was the keyboard
player in David Munrow's Early Music Consort of
London and later founded the Academy of Ancient
Music in London.

When a little finger touches the harpsichord,
producing one small sound, the cycle of wonder and
discovery begins again. Musicians are to be
applauded, celebrated, for brightening the world,
and speaking in musical terms of the majesty of life.

Glossary

Abelard, Peter (1079–1142): French philosopher, theologian, and poet-musician.

Bach, Johann Sebastian (1685–1750): German composer.
Bononcini, Giovanni Battista (1670–1747): Italian composer.

Caccini, Giulio (1545–1618): Italian singer and composer noted for his solo songs in the early Baroque monodic style.
Campra, André (1660–1744): French composer of operatic and sacred music.
Charpentier, Marc-Antoine (1634–1704): French composer of scenic, sacred, and instrumental music.
chifonie: a thirteenth-century French name for the hurdy-gurdy, or *vielle à roue.*
citole: a Medieval instrument, wire-strung and plucked, with a rounded, lutelike front and a flat, guitarlike back. Derived from the Greek kithara and related to the Renaissance cittern.
continuo: a bass line (with or without additional shorthand symbols or "figures" to guide the keyboard player or lutenist in supplying the correct harmonies), which served as foundation and accompaniment to

the upper musical voices. Important in Western art music beginning in the late sixteenth century until the late eighteenth century (and persisting in America through the early decades of the nineteenth).

Corelli, Arcangelo (1653 – 1713): Italian violinist and composer.

cornetto (or *cornett*): a wind instrument, either straight or curved in the arc of a circle, with holes like a recorder and a hollow cup-shaped mouthpiece.

Couperin, François (1668 – 1733): French composer and organist.

crwth: a lyrelike string instrument played with a bow: the term is Welsh and middle English.

darbouk: a drum, generally of pottery or metal with a skin head attached, in elongated gourd or goblet form. Of North African or Middle Eastern origin.

des Prez, Josquin (c. 1440 – 1521): northern French composer of sacred and secular vocal polyphony.

Dowland, John (ca. 1563 – 1626): English lutenist and composer.

Dufay, Guillaume (ca. 1400 – 1474): northern French composer of sacred and secular vocal music.

dulcian: a sixteenth- and seventeenth-century small reed instrument sounding much like a soft-timbre bassoon.

dulcimer: a wire-strung instrument shaped like a shallow closed box, with wooden hammers to strike the strings; popular in fifteenth- and sixteenth-century Britain and still popular in eastern Europe.

Frescobaldi, Girolamo (1583 – 1643): Italian organist and composer.

Froberger, Johann Jakob (1616 – 1667): German organist and composer.

frottola (plural *frottole*): a secular song popular in Italy around the turn of the sixteenth century. Forerunner of the more developed and musically complex *madrigal.*

Gabrieli, Andrea (1520 – 1586): Italian organist and composer.

Gabrieli, Giovanni (1555 – 1612): Italian organist and composer; nephew of Andrea.

gamba (Italian, "leg"): see *viol.*

Geminiani, Francesco (1687 – 1762): Italian violinist and composer.

gemshorn: Medieval flute made from an animal horn, thus shaped in a tapering cone.

Gibbons, Orlando (1583 – 1625): English composer and keyboard player.

Gregorian chant: a codification of the liturgical chant of the Western Christian church; often used interchangeably with the terms *plainchant* and *plainsong.*

Handel, George Frideric (1685 – 1759): English composer, born in Germany.

harpsichord: a keyboard instrument especially popular from the sixteenth to the end of the eighteenth century, similar in shape to the piano, but producing its characteristic sound by the plucking of its strings.

Haydn, Franz Joseph (1732 – 1809): Austrian composer.

Janequin, Clément (ca. 1485 – 1558): French composer noted for his secular chansons.

krumhorn (literally, "crooked horn"): late Medieval wind instrument family with double reeds and cylindrical tubes, recurved at the end.

Landini, Francesco (ca. 1325 – 1397): Italian composer, poet, and performer of the *Ars nova quatrecento* style-period.

Lassus, Roland de (1532 – 1594): Franco-Flemish composer of late Renaissance polyphony.

Lully, Jean-Baptiste (1632 – 1687): French composer, born in Italy.

lute: pear-shaped instrument with a rounded back, popular in England until the mid-eighteenth century; of Arabian origin.

Machaut, Guillaume de (1300 – 1377): French composer and poet.

madrigal: a manner of setting words to music, originating in Italy ca. 1530, in which each new line of poetry is given an autonomous musical setting. The term *madrigal* also occurs in fourteenth-century Italian secular music.

Marais, Marin (1656 – 1728): French composer; reputed to be the best player of the viola da gamba that ever lived.

Marcabru: twelfth-century Gascon troubadour.

Marenzio, Luca (1553 – 1599): Italian singer and composer of madrigals.

monody: music consisting of a single melodic line.

Monteverdi, Claudio (1567 – 1643): Italian composer.

motet: a term employed from the thirteenth through the eighteenth century to denote polyphonic musical composition; in the Renaissance, refers to sacred vocal music.

Mozart, Wolfgang Amadeus (1756 – 1791): Austrian composer.

neume: a sign for a note or group of notes; manuscripts in neumatic notation began appearing in Europe in the ninth century.

organetto: a small portable organ, popular from the thirteenth to the sixteenth century; often appears in fourteenth-century paintings.

oud: a stringed instrument like a lute or mandolin, found in southwest Asia and northern Africa.

Palestrina, Giovanni Pierluigi da (1525–1594): Italian composer.

part-song: used generically to denote secular vocal part-music.

Perotin: twelfth-century French composer of liturgical polyphony.

plainsong: traditional ritual melody of the Western Christian church; synonym for *Gregorian chant.*

Praetorius, Michael (1571–1621): German composer, author of *Syntagma musicum* (1615–1619), an important discussion of the music of the period.

psaltery: a Medieval and Renaissance stringed instrument, played by plucking the strings.

Purcell, Henry (1659–1695): English composer and organist.

Rameau, Jean-Philippe (1683–1764): French composer and introducer of important new theories of harmony.

rauschpfeife: Medieval-Renaissance reed instrument of the shawm family, treble in pitch (see *shawm*).

rebec: one of the earliest bowed instruments, an ancestor of the violin; no longer popular in Europe after the sixteenth century.

recorder (also *flûte douce, flûte à bec; Blockflöte*): name for a family of end-blown vertical flutes, with whistle mouthpieces, ranging in pitch from high treble to contrabass.

Rore, Cipriano de (ca. 1515–1565): Flemish composer active in Italy.

sackbut: early name for the trombrone, prevalent by the fourteenth century in Europe.

saltarello: a jumping dance, probably Tuscan in origin, in triple measure.

Scarlatti, Domenico (1685–1757): Italian composer, especially noted for his harpsichord works.

shawm: Medieval-Renaissance name for a double-reed instrument family, precursors of the oboe.

Susato, Tilman (ca. 1500–ca. 1564): Flemish composer and music publisher.

Tartini, Giuseppe (1692 – 1770): Italian violinist and composer.

Telemann, Georg Philipp (1681 – 1767): German composer.

theorbo: the largest of the lute family (see *lute*).

trotto: Medieval Italian dance in triple time.

trouvères: the northern French poet-musicians who composed secular lyrics in the *langue d'oil,* or Old French.

vielle: Medieval bowed string instrument.

vihuela: a double-strung, six-course guitar popular in Spain during the sixteenth century.

viol or *viola da gamba:* a family of fretted, bowed stringed instruments popular in Europe from the late fifteenth to the mid-eighteenth century.

Vivaldi, Antonio (ca. 1675 – 1741): Italian composer and violinist.

Wilbye, John (1574 – 1638): English madrigalist.

Index

Abelard, Peter, 45; "Planctus," 42
Academy of Ancient Music: eighteenth-century, 13; modern, 213
Academy of Vocal Music, London, 12
Alarius ensemble, 57–59
amateurs, 16, 20, 31, 55, 62, 85–89, 158
Amsterdam Baroque Orchestra, 178, 204
Amsterdam Concertgebouw, 54
Anthologie Sonore, 33
Armstrong, Louis, 92
Armstrong, Nancy, 120–121, 139
Ars Nova, 114
articulation techniques, 5, 42, 48, 52–53, 59, 204
Aston Magna, 193, 197
Aulos ensemble, 193, 201
Austria, 6
"authenticity," 9, 10, 31, 36, 43, 55, 60, 72, 90–95
avant-garde, 4, 7–9, 64, 69

Babitz, Sol, 51
Bach, Johann Sebastian, 3, 15, 26, 43, 47, 48, 65, 68, 69, 78, 91; Brandenburg concerti, 90; Equiluz's performance of vocal music, 81–82; first biography of, 14; instruments for, 49, 52; recordings of works, 52, 53–54, 58; *Saint Matthew Passion,* 12; *Well-Tempered Clavier,* 25
Bagby, Ben, 27, 117
Baker, Sharon, 190
Banchetto Musicale, 136–137, 188
Baroque music, 4, 5, 40, 66, 87; performance of, 15, 20, 24–26, 46–50, 51, 52, 53–54, 57, 58, 59, 62, 63, 65, 68–70, 71, 137, 138, 204; popularity of, 26–27, 101; singing, 53–54, 78, 80, 81–82, 83, 140–141

Bartók, Béla, 87
Bäss, Hajo, 169
bass viol, Baroque, 184–185
Beckett, John, 80, 145
Beethoven, Ludwig van, 60, 65, 66, 83, 86; *Choral Fantasia,* 207
Belgium, Belgian musicians, 57–60
Berio, Luciano, 64
Binkley, Thomas, 27, 34, 38–45, 115
Blake, William, quoted, 50
Boeke, Kees, 64
Boîte à Musique, 78
Bononcini, Giovanni Battista, 12–13
Boston Camerata, 35, 118, 126, 159, 195
Boston Early Music Festival, 23, 24, 125, 150–153, 154–155, 156, 161
Boston Museum Trio, 164, 195, 197
Boston Symphony Orchestra, 212–213
Boulanger, Nadia, 24–25, 78
Boulin, Sophie, 138–139
Bowman, James, 140–141
Brahms, Johannes, 48, 60
Brüggen, Daniël, 180–181
Brüggen, Frans, 4, 54, 60, 61–66, 85, 187, 197, 208–209, 210–211
Bylsma, Anner, 59, 186, 187

Caccini, Giulio, 74
Camerata Trajectina, 134–135
Campbell, Margaret, *Dolmetsch,* quoted, 21, 22n, 96–97
Campra, André, 57, 95
Cape, Safford, 27–28, 33n
Capella Antiqua, Munich, 28
Carmina Burana, 40
Carrai, Phoebe, 169
cello, 187, 190, 191

chansons, 39, 83
Chapelle Royale, Paris, 171
Charpentier, Marc-Antoine, 24
China, 6n
Chopin, Frédéric, 95
Christie, William, 182
church music, 12
citole, 99
clavichord, 19
Clemencic, René, 40n
Clemencic Consort, Vienna, 36
Cobb, Willard, 39
Cohen, Joel, 126
Coleman, Tom, 191
Collegium Musicum, 15–16
Collegium Vocale, Ghent, 171
Concentus Musicus, Vienna, 51–55, 59
Concert of Antient Music, London, 13
Concerto Vocale, 182
concerts, 6–7, 9, 25, 27–28, 29, 32–33, 34, 36, 39, 64, 71, 87, 88, 97, 98–99, 100–101
conservatories, 5, 16, 44, 46, 48, 59, 97–98, 100
Corelli, Arcangelo, 12
cornet, 97
cornetto, 98, 142–143
Couperin, François, 4, 15, 56, 57, 70
Covey-Crump, Rogers, 166–167
crwth, 47
Cuénod, Hugues, 78, 81
Curson, Ted, 123
Cyprus, 107

Dael, Lucy van, 59, 208, 209
darbouk, 41
Das alte Werk, 38
Deller, Alfred, 26, 76–77, 78, 79
Derenne, Paul, 78
des Prez, Josquin, 3, 24, 32, 58, 93–94; *Missa Pange Lingua,* 94
Dickey, Bruce, 142
Dolmetsch, Arnold, 18–23, 25, 31, 40, 51, 73, 97, 98; and recorder, 86–87
Dolmetsch, Hélène, 19n
Dolmetsch Foundation, 21
Donington, Robert, quoted, 18–19, 21
Dopmeyer, Ralph, 155
Dowland, John, 6, 44, 122, 125
Dreyfus, Laurence, quoted, 12, 90, 91, 98–99, 100
Driever, Bertho, 180–181
Dufay, Guillaume, 27, 79
dulcian, 99, 161
dulcimer, 99

Early Music Consort of London, 26, 28, 36, 123, 213
early music revival: beginnings of, 12–14, 96–97; effect of the present on, 28–29, 31, 36n;

explanations of, 4–10; future of, 99–102; performers' backgrounds, 97–98; scholarship and, 14–17, 43–44
Egmond, Max von, 54, 81
England, 6; early music revival in, 12–14; first commercial concert in, 87
English Consort, London, 145, 147
English singers and music, 76, 77, 79, 82–84
Equiluz, Kurt, 54, 81–82
Ericson, Wolf, 38

Figueras, Montserrat, 80
Figueras, Pilar, 80
Fitch, Ken, 118–119
flute, 62, 203; Baroque, 157. *See also* transverse flute
Forkel, Johann Nikolaus, 14
France: controversy about early music in, 3–4, 5, 16, 56, 57; music criticism in, 68; Renaissance Fayre in, 89n
France Musique, 56
Franck, César, 58
French music, 5, 24, 27, 39, 40n, 56–58, 81, 82, 83, 114, 118
Frescobaldi, Girolamo, 68, 109, 110, 186
Froberger, Johann Jakob, "Meditation sur ma mort future," 68
frottole, 39
Fuller, Albert, 196, 197

Gabrieli, Andrea, 11
Gabrieli, Giovanni, 11
Galpin, Francis, 97
gamba. *See* viola da gamba
Gay, John, *Beggar's Opera,* 13
Geminiani, Francesco, 12
gemshorn, 98
George III, 13
German language, 81–82
German monodic music, 40n
Germany, study of early music in, 12, 14–16. *See also individual composers*
Gershwin, George, 60
Gesamtausgabe, 15
Gibbons, John, 164–165, 187, 197
Gibbons, Orlando, 152
Goebel, Reinhard, 168–169
Greenberg, Noah, 26, 28, 29, 30–37, 123
Greenwood Consort, 161
Gregorian chant, 107
Grofé, Ferde, 35n
ground bass, Renaissance, 123

Hamlin, Jessica, 159
Handel, George Frideric, 13, 15, 27, 60, 78, 83; *Messiah,* 178, 204
Hannan, Peter, 179
Harnoncourt, Alice, 51, 59

Harnoncourt, Nikolaus, 3, 4, 51–55, 59, 66n, 69, 81; quoted, 10
harp, Renaissance, 161
harpsichord, 19, 25–26, 68–70, 88, 146–147, 164–165, 214–215
Haslemere, 19n, 21
Hauwe, Walter van, 64
Hawkins, John, 13
Haydn, Franz Joseph, 6, 27, 59, 60, 65, 66, 83, 174
Henderson, Fletcher, 35n
Henry, Michael, 178
Herreweghe, Philippe, 171–173
Hesperion XX, 171
Hicks, Neva, 159
Hilliard Ensemble, 166–167
Hillier, Paul, 166–167
Hindemith, Paul, 8, 16
Hogwood, Christopher, 212–213
Hollander, John, 98
Hopkins, Mark, 158
Hortulani Musicae, 179
Howell, Robin, 200–201
Huelgas Ensemble, 106, 107
Huene, Friedrich von, 157

India, 6n, 80
instruments, period, 5, 55; adaptability of early music to, 34–35n; Baroque, 47–50, 51, 52, 184–185; vs. modern, 49–50, 59, 66n; reproductions of, 19, 20–21, 25, 65, 74, 88, 156–157, 160–161, 190; and singers, 74–75; Studio's, 38, 41–42, 115. *See also specific instruments*
Italian music, 11, 36, 39, 78, 81, 82, 83, 109, 111

Jacobs, René, 182–183
Jaffee, Kay, 129
Jaffee, Michael, 128
Janequin, Clément, 24
jazz, 41, 44, 92
Jeppesen, Laura, 194–195, 197
Jones, Sterling, 27, 38, 39, 42, 113, 114–115
Joyce, James, quoted, 20
Junghaenel, Konrad, 182

Kevy, Sybil, 158
Kirkby, Emma, 82, 83, 109, 110, 112
Kirkpatrick, Ralph, 23–24, 27
Klein, Phyllis, 158
Kohnen, Robert, 57, 58
Koopman, Ton, 204–205
krumhorn, 16, 85, 161
Kuijken brothers, 4, 56, 58, 59–60; Bart, 46, 58, 60, 174; Sigiswald, 46, 57–58, 60, 61, 67, 174, 175; Wieland, 46, 58, 59, 60, 174, 176–177, 195
Kurz, Tom, 158

Landini, Francesco, 101
Landowska, Wanda, 21, 24, 25–26, 27, 61, 69
Lassus, Roland de, 15, 88, 101
Leenhouts, Paul, 180–181
Legvin, Elizabeth, 192, 193
Leonhardt, Gustav, 3, 58, 61, 67–72, 81, 99, 152–153; quoted, 90
Leonhardt, Marie, quoted, 4
Levitt, Richard, 27, 39
Loeki Stardust Quartet, 180–181
London, 148–149
London Classical Players, 206–207
London Consort of Musicke, 109, 110
London Early Music Group, 35, 123
Lully, Jean-Baptiste, 52, 57, 65, 79
lute, 5, 19, 36, 47, 122, 123, 124–125; songs, 79, 110
Lute Society, 125
Lutzke, Myron, 193

McDonald, Lawrence, 198–199
Machaut, Guillaume de, 3, 14, 16, 43, 79, 84
Mackie, Nan, 179
Maddelena, James, 136
Madrigal Society, 13–14
madrigals, 6, 14, 27, 39n, 78, 83, 109, 110; amateurs and, 87–88
Maffei, Giovanni Camillo, quoted, 75n
Mahler, Gustav, 95
Malgoire, Jean-Claude, 57
Marais, Marin, 58; "Le tombeau de Monsieur Blancrocher," 60
Marcabru, 74
Marenzio, Luca, 12, 88
Martin, Anthony, 197
Martin, Steve, 191
Medieval music, 4, 5, 26, 38, 47, 51, 91; monody, 40–41, 44, 79, 117; notation, 40–41, 42; performance of, 27, 28, 30, 31, 32–33, 40–45, 115, 118, 129; polyphony, 5, 43; singing, 41, 42, 44, 78–80, 81, 145
Mendelssohn, Felix, 12, 69
monody, 40–41, 44, 79, 81, 117
Monteverdi, Claudio, 3, 53, 80, 84, 88, 95, 99; *Orfeo*, 54; "Zefiro torna," 78
Middle East, and Medieval music, 41–42, 44
Morley, Rosamund, 129
Morris, William, 98
Morrow, Michael, 80, 144, 145
Morton, Jelly Roll, 92
motets, 107
Mozart, Wolfgang Amadeus, 6, 13, 43, 47, 54–55, 60, 65–66, 190; *Jupiter* symphony, 65; Quintet in A Major, 198
Munrow, David, 26, 28, 29, 36, 123, 141, 213
music societies, 15. *See also individual names*
Musica Antiqua Köln, 169
Musica Reservata, 80, 145

Musical World, quoted, 97
Musicians of Swanne Alley, 122
musicology, 14–17, 43, 94

Nelson, Judith, 182
Netherlands Kamerkoor, 142
neumes, 42
Nevel, Paul van, 107, 108
New Grove's Dictionary of Music and Musicians,
    quoted, 12–13, 68, 93
New York Pro Musica, 28, 30–36, 38, 123
Noorman, Jantina, 80, 145
Norrington, Roger, 206
Norstrom, Lyle, 122
North, Nigel, 127
Northcott, Erica, 179
notation, 15, 40–41, 42
Nurse, Ray, 179

Oberlin, Russell, 32
oboe, Baroque, 81
O'Dette, Paul, 122
Oliver, King, 92
Orchestra of the Eighteenth Century, 54, 65,
    197, 209
Orff, Carl, 40n
organetto, 41, 47
oud, 41, 98

Paganini, Niccolò, 83
Palestrina, Giovanni Pierluigi da, 14, 15, 79, 87
Pan ensemble, 114–115
Papp, Nicolas, 184–185
Parker, Charlie, 187
Pater, Walter, 98
Pavarotti, Luciano, 99
Pearlman, Martin, 188, 189
Pellini, Giovanni, 124, 125
Pepusch, John Christopher, 13
Perotin, 12
Petite Band, La, 58, 59, 60, 67
Pharo, Carol, 121
Philadelphia Baroque Orchestra, 201
Phillips, Caitlin, 159
piccolo trumpet, 123
Pinnock, Trevor, 145, 146–147
pipe, Renaissance, 161
Play of Daniel (Ludus Danielis), 31, 35, 118–
    119, 120–121
Pleyel harpsichords, 25–26
polyphony, 40n, 43, 83, 107
poetry: and Medieval monody, 41; and singing,
    77
Poulton, Diana, 125
Pound, Ezra, 8, 98
Praetorius, Michael, *Syntagma musicum,* 34n
Princeton project, 93–94
Pro Musica Antiqua, Brussels, 27–29, 33n

Provence, 6, 40n, 78, 92
psaltery, 99
Puccini, Giacomo, 78
Purcell, Henry, *Dido and Aeneas,* 81

rackett, 161
Raffensperger, Fred, 118–119
Rameau, Jean-Philippe, 57, 65, 67, 68; *Zoroastre,*
    136–139
Ramm, Andrea von, 3, 38, 39, 79, 118; quoted,
    82
rauschpfeife, 99
rebec, 47, 89n, 89, 115
recorder, 5, 19, 47, 61–64, 85–87, 88, 97, 157,
    161, 181
recordings of early music, 33n, 38, 39–40, 52,
    53–54, 55, 58–59, 61, 84, 100, 141
Renaissance Fayres, 89
Renaissance music, 4, 5, 26, 38, 47, 51, 87;
    adaptability of, 34–35n; performance of, 24,
    27, 28–29, 30, 32, 33–34, 35, 39–40, 51,
    123, 129; and recorder, 62; singing, 14, 78–
    80, 81, 83–84, 145
Richie, Stanley, 197
Riemann, Hugo, 15
Rife, Jean, 190
Riley, Caitlin, 159
Rogers, Nigel, 38, 39, 80, 81, 140
Romantic music, 5, 7, 14, 25, 48, 52, 60, 69, 88
Rooley, Anthony, 109, 110
Rore, Cipriano de, 27
Rubinlicht, Janine, 57, 58, 59, 173
Ruhland, Konrad, 28

Sachs, Curt, 33n
sackbut, 98, 142
Salomon Quartet, London, 145
saltarello, 47
Sandwich, Earl of, 13
Sansom, Roy, 161
Savall, Jordi, 170–171
Scarlatti, Domenico, 23, 98
Schachtman, Marc, 200
Schaeftlein, Jürg, 53
Schoenberg, Arnold, *Pierrot Lunaire,* 4
scholarship, and early music, 14–17, 43–44
Schroeder, Jaap, 198–199
Schumann, Robert, 69, 87
Schütz, Heinrich, *Saint Matthew Passion,* 166–
    167
Schutz Choir, 206–207
Sequentia ensemble, Cologne, 27, 117
Sestetto Luca Marenzio, 33n, 78
Shankar, Ravi, 44
Shaw, George Bernard, 98; quoted, 73, 84
shawm, 9, 98
Silverstein, Steve, 160, 161

singing, early music, 14, 38–39, 41, 42, 44, 53–54, 73–84, 109, 110, 130, 140–141, 145
Sixteen, The, 204
Smith, Hopkinson, 27
Snapp, Shannon, 191
Snellings, Dirk, 106
Snodgrass, W. D., 98
Société des Instruments Anciens, 20
Society of Recorder Players, 22
Solum, John, 202, 203
Sour Cream, 64
Spanish music, 35, 80
Staier, Andreas, 169
Standage, Simon, 145
Starkman, Jane, 201
Stasny, Leopold, 53
Steeb, Karlheinz, 169
Steenhover, Karel van, 180–181
Stepner, Daniel, 188, 197
Stich-Randall, Theresa, 78
Stravinsky, Igor, 8; *Le sacre du printemps,* 4
Studio der Fruehen Musik, Munich, 27, 38–40, 43–45, 79, 80, 114–115, 117
Susato, Tilman, 98
Sutherland, Joan, 82
Sylvan, Sanford, 136–137

tabor, 161
Tagliavini, Luigi-Ferdinando, 154, 155
tambourine, 35, 42
Tan, Melvin, 206
Tartini, Giuseppe, 101
Tchaikowsky, Peter Ilich, 83
Telefunken, 61
Telemann, Georg Philipp, 58, 62, 64, 101
theorbo, 98
Thomas, David, 80, 130–131
Thorndike, Sybil, quoted, 18
Thornton, Barbara, 27, 116–117
Tindemans, Margrit, 117

Titanic Records, 155, 186
transverse flute, 60, 61, 62, 86, 157
trotto, 47
troubadours, 6, 8; songs, 41, 44, 74, 81
trouvère songs, 44, 79
Tubb, Evelyn, 110
Turkovic, Milan, 53
Tyler, James, 27, 123

universities, and early music, 14–16, 100
Utrecht Early Music Festival, 59–60, 162–163, 164–165, 172–173, 174, 178, 179

Vasto, Chanterelle del, 78
Ventadorn, Bernard de, 44
Verdi, Giuseppe, 48, 78, 99
Veronese, Paolo, *Marriage at Cana,* 184
vielle, 42, 47, 52, 89n, 98, 115, 117, 156, 195
Vienna Symphony Orchestra, 53
vihuela da mano, 98, 156
viola da gamba, 9, 19, 47, 52, 58, 60, 98, 195
violin, 19, 61, 70; Baroque, 5, 47, 48–49, 51, 81, 145, 169, 173
Vivaldi, Antonio, 4, 14, 53, 57, 65, 101; *Four Seasons,* 188, 190

Wagner, Richard, *Die Meistersinger,* 40n
Waverly Consort, New York, 35, 128–129
Wesley, Samuel, 12
Whore of Babylon, The, 132–135
Wilbye, John, 88
Wilson, Christopher, 125
Wizansky, Sasha, 159

Yeats, William Butler, 8

Zukof, Katie, 159
Zukof, Larry, 159
Zurich opera orchestra, 54
Zwang, Doctor, 4, 101